2

CANADIAN GRAMMAR SPECTRUM

REFERENCE AND PRACTICE

Harrison

OXFORD
UNIVERSITY PRESS

OXFORD
UNIVERSITY PRESS

Oxford University Press is a department of the University of Oxford.
It furthers the University's objective of excellence in research, scholarship, and education by publishing worldwide.
Oxford is a registered trade mark of Oxford University Press in the UK and in certain other countries.

Published in Canada by
Oxford University Press
8 Sampson Mews, Suite 204,
Don Mills, Ontario M3C 0H5 Canada

www.oupcanada.com

First Edition Published in 2012

Oxford Practice Grammar was originally published in 2006. This edition is published by arrangement with Oxford University Press, Great Clarendon Street, Oxford OX2 6DP, United Kingdom.

Library and Archives Canada Cataloguing in Publication

Harrison, Mark, 1955-
Canadian grammar spectrum 2 : reference and practice / Mark Harrison.

Includes index.
Previously published as part of: Coe, Norman.
Oxford practice grammar.
Basic, 2006.
ISBN 978-0-19-544705-7

1. English language—Grammar—Problems, exercises, etc.
2. English language—Textbooks for second language learners.
I. Coe, Norman. Oxford practice grammar. Basic. II. Title.

PE1128.H36 2011 428.2'4 C2011-900737-1

Oxford University Press is committed to our environment.
This book is printed on Forest Stewardship Council® certified paper, harvested from responsible sources.

FSC
www.fsc.org
MIX
Paper from responsible sources
FSC® C004071

Printed and bound in Canada.

3 4 — 16 15

Contents

Reported speech

Articles, nouns, pronouns, etc.

Adjectives and adverbs

Prepositions

Building sentences

Appendices

Introduction

Canadian Grammar Spectrum is a series of books, each written at the appropriate level for you at each stage in your study of English. The series is intended for your use either in a classroom or when working independently on your own time.

The books are divided into two-page units, each of which covers an important grammar topic. Each unit starts with an explanation of the grammar and is followed by a set of practice exercises. A test at the end of each book gives the opportunity for more practice and enables you to assess how much you have learned. Answers to the exercises and the tests are provided at the back of the book.

You may want to choose the order in which you study the grammar topics, perhaps going first to those which are giving you problems. (Topics are listed in the Contents page at the front of each book and in the Index at the back.) Alternatively, you may choose to start at the beginning of each book and work through to the end.

Key to symbols

The symbol / (oblique stroke) between two words means that either word is possible. *We write **does** before **he/she/it*** means that *We write **does** before **he***, *We write **does** before **she***, and *We write **does** before **it*** are all possible. In exercise questions, this symbol is also used to separate words or phrases which are possible answers.

Parentheses ( ) around a word or phrase in the middle of a sentence mean that it can be left out. *She said (that) she lived in a small apartment* means that there are two possible sentences: *She said that she lived in a small apartment* and *She said she lived in a small apartment*.

The symbol ~ means that there is a change of speaker. In the example *When did Jane go to India? ~ In June*, the question and answer are spoken by different people.

The symbol ▶ in an exercise indicates that a sample answer is given.

Simple Present

1 We form the Simple Present like this:

POSITIVE	
Singular	I **know**
	you **know**
	he/she/it **knows**
Plural	we **know**
	you **know**
	they **know**

*I **know** the answer.*
*She **starts** work at 9:30.*

We add **-s** after **he/she/it:**

I start → he start**s**	I live → she live**s**

If a verb ends in **-ch**, **-o**, **-sh**, or **-ss**, we add **-es** after **he/she/it:**

I watch → he watch**es**	you do → he do**es**
they go → it go**es**	we wash → she wash**es**

If a verb ends in a consonant (**b**, **c**, etc.) + **y** (e.g. **study**), we use **-ies** after **he/she/it:**

I study → he stud**ies**	I fly → it fl**ies**

(For more examples, see Appendix 2, page 95.)

2 Now look at these examples of the negative:

*I **don't like** that music.*
*He **doesn't listen** to his teacher.*

NEGATIVE *FULL FORM*	*SHORT FORM*
I **do not know.**	I **don't know.**
You **do not know.**	You **don't know.**
He/She/It **does not know.**	He **doesn't know.**
We **do not know.**	We **don't know.**
You **do not know.**	You **don't know.**
They **do not know.**	They **don't know.**

Note that we say:
He does not know. (NOT ~~*He does not knows.*~~)

3 We use the Simple Present:

- to talk about things that happen regularly:
  *He **plays** golf every day.*
- to talk about facts:
  *She **comes** from France.*
  (= She is French.)
  *Markets **sell** vegetables.*
  *I **don't speak** Chinese.*

Practice

A Add *-s* or *-es* to the verbs in the sentences if it is necessary. If it is not necessary, put a check (✓) in the blank.

► He work *s*...... in a bank.
► They live *✓*...... in Colombia.
1 She visit .... her aunt on weekends.
2 We watch .... this show all the time.
3 I play .... tennis in the summer.
4 We go .... camping in Algonquin Park.
5 He sing .... in a choir.
6 They always eat .... organic food.
7 I sleep .... late on Saturdays.
8 My boss call .... me often.

B Now complete these sentences using a verb from the box. Use each verb once. Remember to add *-s* or *-es* if necessary.

teach	enjoy	walk	own	~~eat~~	read	fly	finish

► He *eats*......... oatmeal for breakfast.
1 He .... a bookstore downtown.
2 Marcie .... watching scary movies.
3 She .... school at six o'clock.
4 I .... to work for exercise.
5 My brother .... one book every week.
6 She .... at the local high school.
7 We .... to Mexico in the winter.

C Write these sentences, using the negative form of the Simple Present.

► (He/not/live/in Mexico) He doesn't live in Mexico.
1 (We/not/speak/German) ....
2 (My dog/not/get/enough exercise) ....
3 (He/not/eat/beef) ....
4 (I/not/play/badminton) ....
5 (You/not/sing/very well) ....
6 (They/not/cook/often) ....
7 (She/not/hear/the music) ....
8 (I/not/understand/the question) ....

D Write the verbs from the box in the Simple Present. Use each verb once.

leave	start	arrive	~~get~~	watch	work	brush
eat	have	like	drink	go	stop	

Interviewer: How do you start the day, Jim?
Jim: Well, I (►) get............ up at six o'clock. I shower and dress, and I (1)................ breakfast at seven o'clock. After breakfast, I (2)................ my teeth. I (3)................ to work at quarter to eight.
Interviewer: When do you get to work?
Jim: I usually (4)................ at my office at about eight o'clock. First, I (5)................ a cup of coffee, and then I (6)................ work at 8:15 a.m.
Interviewer: Where do you work?
Jim: I (7)................ in a bank. I am a computer technician. I (8)................ my job. It's very interesting.
Interviewer: When do you eat lunch?
Jim: I (9)................ work and I have lunch at one o'clock. I (10)................ a cup of coffee at three-thirty.
Interviewer: When do you finish work?
Jim: I (11)................ the office at six o'clock. I eat dinner when I get home. Then I (12)................ TV for an hour or two.

E Use the table to write facts about Joan. A check (✓) means that something is true. An X (✗) means that something is not true. Use the verbs in parentheses ( ).

►	1	2	3	4
from Taiwan ✓	in a factory ✗	in a city ✓	French ✓	surfing ✗
from Mexico ✗	in a bakery ✓	in the country ✗	Japanese ✗	cycling ✓

► (come) She comes from Taiwan. ► She doesn't come from Mexico.
1 (work) She .... in a factory. She .... in a bakery.
2 (live) She .... She ....
3 (speak) ....
4 (like) ....

Present Progressive

1 We form the Present Progressive like this:

be + -ing form
I am eating.

Here are the forms of the Present Progressive:

POSITIVE

FULL FORM	*SHORT FORM*
I **am eating**.	**I'm eating**.
You **are eating**.	**You're eating**.
He/She/It **is eating**.	**He's eating**.
We **are eating**.	**We're eating**.
You **are eating**.	**You're eating**.
They **are eating**.	**They're eating**.

NEGATIVE

FULL FORM	*SHORT FORM*
I **am not** eating.	**I'm not** eating.
You **are not** eating.	You **aren't** eating.
He/She/It **is not** eating.	He **isn't** eating.
We **are not** eating.	We **aren't** eating.
You **are not** eating.	You **aren't** eating.
They **are not** eating.	They **aren't** eating.

2 To make the **-ing** form, we add **-ing** to the verb:

listen → listening	play → playing
work → working	read → reading

3 But notice these irregular spellings:

win → winning	get → getting
shop → shopping	sit → sitting
swim → swimming	travel → travelling
dance → dancing	write → writing
shine → shining	

(For more details on the spelling of the **-ing** form, see Appendix 2, page 95.)

4 We use the Present Progressive:

► to talk about actions and situations in progress now:

► to talk about actions and situations in progress around now, but not exactly at the moment we speak:

Practice

A Look at these pictures.

►

1

2

3

4

Decide what is happening (✓) and what isn't happening (✗) in each picture, and then write positive or negative sentences.

►	(George/eat/breakfast)	✗	*George isn't eating breakfast.*
	(George/sleep)	✓	*George is sleeping.*
1	(They/eating dinner)	....	....
	(They/relaxing)	....	....
2	(I/do homework)	....	....
	(I/talk/to a friend on the phone)	....	....

3 (They/play/tennis) | .... | ....
(They/play/soccer) | .... | ....
4 (We/enjoy/a day at the beach) | .... | ....
(It/rain) | .... | ....

B Finish the postcard using the words in parentheses ( ) in the Present Progressive. Use full forms (e.g. *is sitting*).

Dear Mom and Dad,

Sarah and I (▶) are enjoying................ (enjoy) our trip. We (1)........................ (stay) at a beautiful hotel right by the beach and we (2)........................ (swim) in the ocean every day. Sarah (3)........................ (walk) on the beach every morning to enjoy the sunrise, while I (4)........................ (sleep) in. I (5)........................ (take) lots of pictures with my new camera and Sarah (6)..................... (write) in her journal in the evenings. Right now, the sun (7)........................ (shining) and lots of people (8)........................ relax on the beach. I (9)........................ (try) to finish all my postcards quickly so I can join them!

Tony

C Match the two halves of the sentences. Then write the correct form of the verb in parentheses ( ).

▶ My aunt is staying........... (stay) with us this week
1 The weather is nice
2 We .... (take) a long vacation
3 My brother and I .... (cook) for the family this week
4 Thomas needs to start studying more
5 My dad .... (buy) new golf clubs
6 The students .... (work) on a project
7 Susan left work early

a because he .... (fail) his classes.
b so they will be up late.
c because she .... (go) to a doctor's appointment.
d so I am sleeping......... (sleep) in the living room.
e so I .... (walk) to work this week.
f because he .... (retire) this year.
g because my mom is away.
h because we won some money in the lottery.

▶ d...... 1 .... 2 .... 3 .... 4 .... 5 .... 6 .... 7 ....

Simple Present or Present Progressive

Compare the Simple Present and the Present Progressive:

1 We use the Simple Present to talk about facts (things which are true at any time):

*Anna **speaks** good Mandarin.*
*Journalists **write** newspaper articles.*
*I **come** from Norway.* (= I am Norwegian).

We use the Present Progressive to talk about actions in progress at the time of speaking:

*Anna's busy. She's **speaking** on the phone.*
*What **are you writing**? ~ A letter to Jane.*
*Look! The bus **is coming**.*

2 We use the Simple Present for situations that exist over a long time, and for actions that are repeated (e.g. people's habits, or events on a timetable):

*Mike **works** for an advertising company.*
*He **lives** in Vancouver.* (= His home is in Vancouver.)

*Jane **travels** a lot for her job.*
*I **play** a lot of sports.*

We can use words like **usually, often, every**:

*We **usually go** out to dinner on weekends.*
*I **often go** to baseball games on Sundays.*
*The buses **leave every** hour.*

We use the Present Progressive for things that continue for a limited period of time around now (e.g. vacations, visits, temporary jobs, school or university courses):

*John **is working** in the US for six months.*
*He's **living** in New York.*

*Jane's **travelling** around Europe for a month.*
*I'm **doing** a one-year course in tourism.*
*We're **painting** the apartment.*

3 We use the Simple Present with thinking and feeling verbs (e.g. **know, forget, notice, understand, recognize, remember, like, love, hate, want, prefer, need**):

*I **don't know** which train to catch.*

We do not usually use the Present Progressive with thinking and feeling verbs:

NOT ~~*I'm knowing someone who lives in Venice.*~~

4 We use **have** in the Simple Present to talk about possession:

*I **have** a new car.*

We use **think** in the Simple Present to express opinions:

*I **think** she's interesting.*

We use **have** and **think** in the Present Progressive to talk about actions:

*I'm **having** fun.*
*He can't come, he's **having** dinner at the moment.*
*I **am thinking** about my work.*

Practice

A Complete the sentences with the Simple Present (*I do*) or the Present Progressive (*I am doing*).

► I leave.................. (leave) home at seven o'clock every morning.
1 I never .... (take) the bus to work but today my car .... (not work).
2 He .... (eat) toast for breakfast every morning.
3 John and Sarah .... (leave) for Montreal right now.
4 We .... (talk) about going on vacation, but we never .... (go).
5 You .... (study) too much for this quiz.

6 My father .... (walk) the dog twice a day because they both .... (need) the exercise.

7 I .... (be) excited because I .... (start) a new project at work.

8 Why .... (you/sleep) so late on the weekends?

9 We .... (go) to the movies every Friday and this week we .... (eat) dinner at a new restaurant before the movie.

10 What .... (you/do) at the moment? I .... (need) some help if you .... (have) time.

B This is Julio's first letter in English to Samantha. There are some mistakes in it. Cross out the incorrect forms and write in the correct form. Put a check (✓) if the form of the verb is correct.

Dear Samantha,

I **live** (▶) ✓.............. in Mexico with my family. My mother ~~**is teaching**~~ (▶) teaches...... at the university and my father **is being** (1)................ a lawyer. I **have** (2)................ two younger brothers who **live** (3)................ at home and an older sister who **is living** (4)................ in Canada. At the moment my sister, Anna, **studies** (5)................ English at a university in Toronto. I **am wanting** (6)................ to move to Canada someday.

I **am working** (7)................ very hard every day at school, but I **have** (8)................ hobbies for when I **am wanting** (9)................ to relax. I **enjoy** (10)................ playing sports. I **am playing** (11)................ soccer every weekend with my friends.

While I **write** (12)................ this letter, I **have** (13)................ a snack. My younger brothers **watch** (14)................ television in the other room, but they **are not understanding** (15)................ the English shows. I **am being** (16)................ proud of myself because I **understand** (17)................ most of the words.

Please write back soon,
Julio

C Write the sentences using the Simple Present or the Present Progressive.

▶ (Usually she/work/at the office, but this week she/work/at home.)
Usually she works at the office, but this week she's working at home.........................

1 (Suzanne/be/always careful when driving because she/not/want/to have an accident.)
....

2 (Please leave me alone! I/study/for an exam.)
....

3 (Usually I/prefer/to cook at home but I/be/too tired tonight, so we/go/to a restaurant.)
....

4 (John/walk/to school today although he/usually/take/the bus.)
....

5 (you/speak/fluent English?)
....

6 (Everyone/have/fun at the party and no one/want/to leave.)
....

7 (We/practise/verb forms tonight because we/have/an exam tomorrow.)
....

8 (Jane/travel/every summer. Right now, she/tour/South America.)
....

Simple Past

1 We form the Simple Past of regular verbs by adding **-ed** to the verb:

walk → walked	watch → watched
open → opened	ask → asked

There are some exceptions:

- verbs ending with -e:

+ -d:	live → lived	like → liked

- verbs ending with a consonant and -y:

-y → -ied:	apply → applied try → tried

- most verbs ending with one vowel and one consonant:

-p → -pped:	stop → stopped plan → planned

(For more details on the form of the Simple Past, see Appendix 2, page 95.)

2 Many verbs have an irregular Simple Past form:

do → did	have → had
take → took	buy → bought
come → came	stand → stood
find → found	ring → rang
go → went	say → said

(For more details, see Appendix 3, page 96.)

3 We form the negative with **didn't** and the infinitive (e.g. **do, take, understand**):

*I **didn't understand**.* (NOT ~~didn't understood~~)

We form questions with **did** and the infinitive (e.g. **watch**):

***Did** you **watch** the movie?*

4 We use the Simple Past to talk about an action or situation in the past which is finished. We often say when it happened (e.g. **yesterday, last night**):

*Chris **called** me **yesterday**. He **wanted** to ask me something.*
***Did** you **enjoy** the concert **last night**?*

5 We can use the Simple Past with **for** to talk about something that continued for a period of time, and ended in the past:

*I **lived** in Rome **for two years**. Then I went to work in Japan.*

past 1 2 3 4 → now
for 2 years

Practice

A Put a check (✓) next to the correct forms of the Simple Past, and cross out those which are incorrect. You can look at Appendix 3, page 96, before you do the exercise.

became ✓	played	sold	sayed	wanted	swimmed
catched	reminded	freezed	worked	builded	buyed
talked	built	thinked	took	wrote	flied
married	shared	taked	gived	hitted	selled
understood	brought	flew	forgetted	watched	talked
knowed	shut	slept	showed	quitted	came
breaked	drinked	smiled	cutted	thought	knew

B Complete the sentences using the Simple Past form and the words in parentheses ( ).

- We *went*.......... (go) on vacation in Chile last year.

1 James .... (marry) Melissa in June.
2 She .... (catch) the flu and .... (is) sick all weekend.

3 I .... (quit) my job last Monday but I .... (get) a new job on Wednesday and I .... (start) work on Friday.
4 Suzanne .... (bake) a cake last night and .... (bring) it to work this morning.
5 Samantha .... (take) lots of pictures on her vacation but she .... (not/write) in her journal very much.
6 A: .... (you/go) to Costa Rica last year?
B: No, I .... (go) two years ago.
7 A: .... (you/have) a good day at the beach?
B: Yes, the sun .... (shine) all day and we .... (swim) in the ocean.
8 A: .... (your parents/visit) you this weekend?
B: Yes, they .... (come) on Friday and we .... (see) a show on Saturday.

C Write sentences using the correct form of the Simple Past.

► (When/you/leave/the party?) When did you leave the party?..............................
1 (Why/you/stay up so late studying?)
....
2 (I/read/a great book last week, but I/not/remember/the name of it)
....
3 (you/see the hockey game last night?)
....
4 (David/forget/about the plans we made so he/be/late for dinner)
....
5 (I/sell/my house in the city last year and I/buy/a new one in the country)
....
6 (Mark/pay/for his friend's dinner, because his friend/not/have/his wallet)
....

D It's the end of the semester at university. Jack is asking his friend Sarah about her year. Complete their conversation using the correct Simple Past form of the words in parentheses ( ).

Jack: So, (►) did you enjoy........ (you/enjoy) your first year of university?
Sarah: Yes, I (1)...................... (like) most of my classes and I (2)...................... (love) living in residence.
Jack: Most of your classes? (3)...................... (you/enjoy) some classes more than others?
Sarah: Well, I (4)...................... (take) a philosophy class that I (5)...................... (find) very difficult. I (6)...................... (study) hard every night for that. But my math class (7)...................... (be) quite easy so I (8)...................... (not/study) as much for it.
Jack: And you (9)...................... (love) living in residence? That's great!
Sarah: Well, actually, I (10)...................... (have) a roommate at the beginning of the year who (11)...................... (be) difficult to live with. She (12)...................... (listen) to music very loud and she never (13)...................... (clean) up after herself. But we (14)...................... (request) a room change and I (15)...................... (get) a more compatible roommate. We (16)...................... (become) very good friends.

Past Progressive

1 We form the Past Progressive like this:

POSITIVE

I/He/She/It	**was**	**waiting.**
You/We/They	**were**	**waiting.**

NEGATIVE

	FULL FORM	SHORT FORM	
I/He/She/It	**was not**	**wasn't**	**waiting.**
You/We/They	**were not**	**weren't**	**waiting.**

QUESTIONS

Was I/he/she/it	**waiting?**
Were you/we/they	**waiting?**

(For rules on the spelling of -ing forms (e.g. **waiting**), see Appendix 2, page 95.)

2 Look at this example:

A: *What **were** you **doing** at seven o'clock last night?*

B: *I **was driving** home from work.*

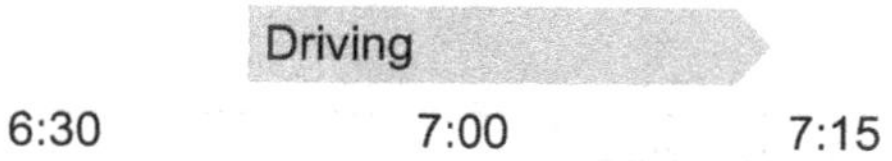

*I **was living** in Japan in 2010. (I lived there from 2008 to 2012.)*

We use the Past Progressive for an action or situation that was in progress at a particular time in the past (e.g. at seven p.m., in 2010).

3 Now look at this:

*When I **walked** into the room, Ann **was writing** postcards and Keith **was reading**.*

We use the Simple Past (**walked**) for a completed action. We use the Past Progressive (**was writing**) for an action in progress in the past.

4 We can use **when** or **while** before the Past Progressive:

*I met her **when/while** we **were working** for the same company.* (**when** = *during the time*)

We can only use **when** (NOT ~~**while**~~) before the Simple Past:

***When** I **met** her, we were working for the same company.* (**when** = *at the time*)

Practice

A **Complete the sentences by changing the verbs in parentheses ( ) into the Past Progressive.**

► It was snowing......... (snow) when I left home this morning.

1 I tried to explain my problem to her, but she .... (not/listen).

2 He .... (talk) on the phone when I arrived.

3 A lot of people .... (wait) for the seven-thirty bus last night.

4 I .... (live) in Victoria when I met them.

5 I nearly had an accident this morning. A car .... (come) towards me, but I moved quickly out of the way.

6 At the end of the first half of the game, they .... (win).

7 It was a sunny afternoon and people .... (sit) on the grass in the park. Then it suddenly started to rain.

8 Which hotel .... (you/stay) in when you lost your passport?

9 Fortunately, I .... (not/drive) too fast when the child walked into the road in front of me.

10 I looked out of the window, and I saw that it .... (not/rain) any more.

11 What .... (you/do) at three o'clock yesterday afternoon?

B Describe what the people in the picture were doing when Rick came into the room. Use the correct verb from the box in the Past Progressive.

brush	watch	~~read~~
listen	write	eat
paint	sit	play

► George was reading......... a newspaper.

1 Julie .... a sandwich.

2 Sue and Liz .... table tennis.

3 Frank .... television.

4 Caroline .... on the floor.

5 Barbara .... a letter.

6 Rita .... her hair.

7 Alison .... to some music.

8 Ann .... a picture.

C Look at this information about Shirley and Kevin and complete the sentences about them, using the Past Progressive (*I was doing*) or the Simple Past (*I did*).

SHIRLEY	
2000–2006	lived in Sherbrooke
2003–2006	studied at university
2006	finished university
2006–2010	worked as a translator
2009	met Kevin
2011	married Kevin

KEVIN	
2002–2010	lived in Thunder Bay
2003–2005	took a course in baking
2005–2010	worked as a baker's assistant
2009	met Shirley
2010–2013	ran his own company
2011	married Shirley

► In 2002 Shirley was living.................... in Sherbrooke.

1 In 2004 Kevin .... in Thunder Bay.

2 In 2004 Shirley .... at university.

3 In 2004 Kevin .... a course in baking.

4 When Shirley .... university in 2006, Kevin .... as a baker's assistant.

5 When Kevin .... Shirley, she .... as a translator.

6 While Shirley .... as a translator, she .... Kevin.

7 In 2011 Kevin .... his own company.

8 While he .... his own company, Kevin .... Shirley.

Present Perfect (1)

1 We use the Present Perfect to talk about something that happened in the past, but we do not say exactly when it happened:

*I've **seen** this movie before.* (= before now)

We often use the Present Perfect in this way for things that happened in the past, and that have a result now:

*I've **seen** this movie before. I don't want to see it again now.*
*She's **left** the company. She doesn't work there now.*

We often use the Present Perfect with **ever** (= at any time) and **never** (= at no time):

*Have you **ever** met a famous person?*
*He has **never** worked in a factory.*

2 We can use the Present Perfect with **for** and **since** to talk about situations or actions in a period of time from the past until now. We use **for** with a period of time (e.g. **three months**), and **since** with a point in time (e.g. **Tuesday**):

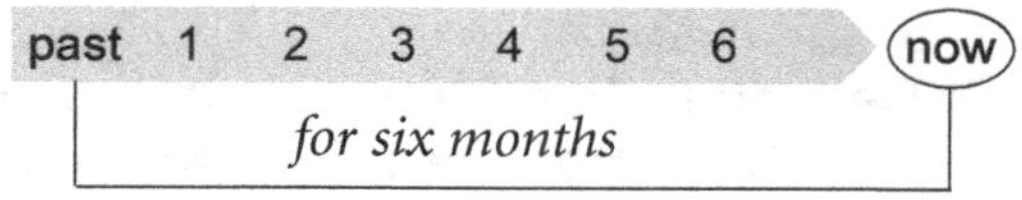

*We've lived here **for six months.***

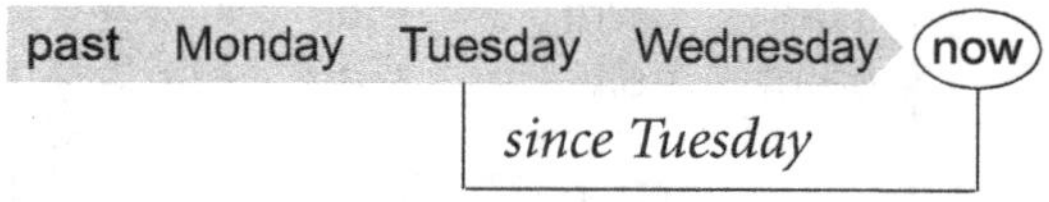

*I haven't seen Tom **since Tuesday.***

3 **Gone and been**
Look at the difference between these two sentences:

*He's **been** to Paris.* (= He is now at home again.)
*He's **gone** to Paris.* (= He is in Paris now.)

He's been means "he has finished his trip."
He's gone means "he has begun his trip."

Practice

A Look at the pictures that show what Sun has done in her life. Complete the sentences about her, using the Present Perfect form of the verbs in parentheses ( ).

► She has been .... (be) mountain climbing.
1 She has been .... (be) married since 1995.
2 She has taught .... (teach) at an elementary school.
3 She has visited .... (visit) Paris every year since university.
4 She has travelled .... (travel) to China.
5 She has worked .... (work) from home as a freelancer.

B Complete the sentences using the Present Perfect form of the verbs in parentheses ( ).

► Don't take my plate away. I haven't finished (not/finish) my meal.

1 A: Which movie do you think will win the Oscar for Best Picture?
B: I don't know. I haven't seen (not/see) any of them.

2 Tom and Joanne have been (be) in Europe for the last three months.

3 A: have you finished (you/finish) studying for your exam?
B: No, I haven't started (not/start) to study. I have been (be) sick for a week.

4 We have travelled (travel) most of the world, but we have never visited (never/visit) Northern Canada.

5 She has written (write) a letter to her mom every week since she moved away.

6 No one have ever beaten (ever/beat) Jim at tennis.

7 Elizabeth has made (make) the cake for all family birthdays for the last two years.

C Write this conversation using the Present Perfect and the words in parentheses ( ).

Ryan: (you/ever/travel/abroad?)

► Have you ever travelled abroad?

Candace: (Yes/I/visit/24 different countries)

1 Yes, I have visited 24 different countries

(But/I/never/spend/more than two weeks in any country)

2 But I never have spended more tha two weeks...

Ryan: (So/you/never/want to live abroad?)

3 so you never have wanted to live abroad

Candace: (No/I/think/about it/but/I/be/unsure about living so far from my family and friends)

4 No I haven't tinke about it but been...

Ryan: (I understand. I/live/in Italy, in Korea, and in Costa Rica)

5 I understand, I have lived in italy, in korea, ...

(At first it was stressful to move, but I/find/it gets easier every time)

6 At first it was stressful to move, but I have finded it gets ...

(I/always/make/great friends wherever I go!)

7 I have always made great friend...

D Write sentences with the Present Perfect and *for* or *since*.

► (I/not/play/lacrosse/last summer.)
I haven't played lacrosse since last summer.

1 (They/work/together/1993.)
They have worked together since 1993

2 (Jack/be/sick/a week.)
Jack has been sick for a week

3 (you/take/many pictures/you bought your new camera?)
you have taked many ... since you have bought

4 (Jennifer/not/see/her sister/she moved across the country.)
Jennifer hasn't say her sister since she has moved

5 (I/not/ride/a bike/five years.)
I haven't ride a bike for five years

Present Perfect (2)

1 We use **just** with the Present Perfect to talk about things that happened a short time before now:

> **have** + **just** + PAST PARTICIPLE
> *It has **just finished**.*

*Could I speak to Su, please? ~ I'm afraid **she has just left**.*
(= She left a short time ago.)
*Is that a good book? ~ I don't know. I've **just started** it.*
(= I started it a short time before now.)

2 Look at this example with **already**:
*Do you want something to eat? ~ No thanks, **I've already eaten**.*
(= I ate before now.)

We use **already** with the Present Perfect to emphasize that something happened before now, or before it was expected to happen. We use **already** like this:

> **have** + **already** + PAST PARTICIPLE
> *I've **already** heard that story.*

Here is another example:
Nicola: *Is Sarah going to call you later?*
Robert: *No. She's* (= She has) ***already** called me.*
(= Sarah called before Nicola expected her to call.)

3 We use **yet** with a negative verb to say that something has not happened, but we think that it will happen:

*The mail **hasn't arrived yet**.*
(= The mail has not arrived, but it probably will arrive.)
***I haven't finished** this work **yet**.*
(= I haven't finished this work, but I will finish it.)
*They **haven't replied** to my email **yet**.*

We use **yet** in questions to ask whether something that we expect to happen has happened:
***Have you paid** the bill **yet**?*
(= Perhaps you have not paid the bill, but you are going to pay it soon.)
***Has it stopped** raining **yet**?*
(= Perhaps it has not stopped raining, but it will stop raining soon.)
***Have you found** a job **yet**?*

Notice that we usually put **yet** at the end of a negative statement or question:
*They haven't replied to my email **yet**.*
*Have you found a job **yet**?*

Practice

A **Complete the dialogues, using *just* and the words in parentheses ( ). Use the Present Perfect.**

► A: What's happening in this movie?
B: I don't know. It's just started.......... (It/start).

1 A: I just came......... (I/come) back from my vacation.
B: Did you have a good time?

2 A: Could I have a copy of *Sports World*, please?
B: Sorry. ...I...just sold....... (I/sell) the last copy.

3 A: How's Lucy?
B: She's very happy. ..she just....finished (She/finish) her exams.

4 A: I just...got............. (I/get) an email from Mike.
B: Oh yes? What did he say?

5 A: Have you heard from Alison and Frank recently?
B: Yes, they just moved (they/move) to another town.
6 A: Do you still have the same car?
B: No, I just bought (I/buy) a new one.
7 A: Would you like something to eat?
B: No, thanks. I just had (I/have) breakfast.

B Write sentences using the Present Perfect with *already* or *yet*.

► (I/not/read/today's newspaper) yet.
I haven't read today's newspaper yet.
1 (you/decide/which one to buy) yet?
you have decided wich one
2 (I/explain/this to you three times) already.
I have explained this to you 3 time already
3 (Their baby son/start/talking) already.
Their baby son have start talked al re
4 (you/call/Lan) yet?
have you called Lan yet?
5 (The game/not/finish) yet.
the game hasn't finished yet.
6 (I/have/lunch) already.
I already have lunch
7 (He/spend/all his money) already.
he have spent all his money already.

C Complete the conversation using *just*, *already*, or *yet* and the words in parentheses ( ). Change the verbs into the Present Perfect.

Julia: Are you having a good time here?
Anna: Yes, I haven't been here long, and (►) I've already visited (I/visit) a lot of interesting places.
Julia: (1) have you visited (you/visit/the art gallery/?)
Anna: No, (2) I haven't do that (I/not/do/that), but I'm going to do it.
Julia: What about the theatre? (3) .... (you/see/a play/?)
Anna: No, but (4) I have buy ticket (I/buy/a ticket) for one. It's called *The Friends*. I called the theatre five minutes ago. already Would you like to come with me?
Julia: Thanks, but (5) .... (I/see/that play). I saw it last month.
Anna: (6) .... (I/read) in the newspaper that The Adventurers are going to play a concert next week. Do you like them?
Julia: Yes, I do. (7) .... (they/release) a really good new album. It came out a couple of days ago.
Anna: I really want to get a ticket.
Julia: (8) .... (they/not/sell/all the tickets). But be quick! They're a very popular band.

Simple Past or Present Perfect

Compare the Simple Past and the Present Perfect:

1 We use the Simple Past to talk about something that happened at a particular time in the past:

*I **met** Vincenzo **at four o'clock**.*
*When **did** Jane go to India? ~ **In June**.*
*Martin **bought** a new car **last week**.*

We use the Present Perfect to talk about the past, but not about when things happened:

*I**'ve met** Vincenzo's girlfriend. She's nice.*
***Have** you ever **been** to India? ~ Yes, I have.*
*I **have** never **bought** a new car.*

2 We use the Simple Past for situations or actions during a period of time that ENDED in the past:

*I **worked** there **for two years.** I left last year.*

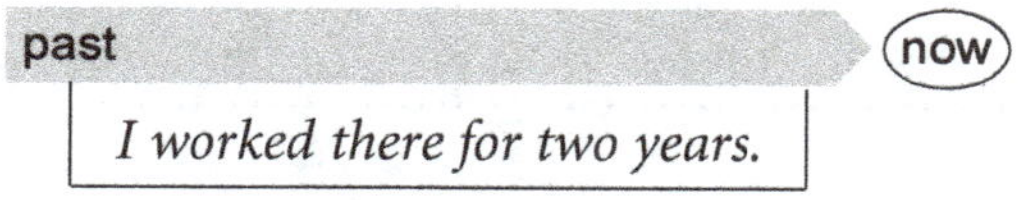

*We **lived** in that house **for a long time**; then we moved to this one.*
*Our company **opened** two new stores **last summer.***

We use the Present Perfect for situations or actions during a period of time from the past to NOW:

*He **has worked** here **for two years.***
(He still works here.)

*We**'ve lived** in this apartment **since we got married.*** (We still live in it.)
*We opened two stores last summer. **Since then*** (= since that time), *we **have opened** two more.*

3 Notice how we often move from the Present Perfect to the Simple Past:

Peter: ***Have** you ever **played** this game before?*
Maria: *Yes, I **played** it once when I was in Alberta.*
Peter: ***Did** you win?*
Maria: *No, I **lost**.*

Practice

A **Complete the conversation by choosing the correct form in parentheses ( ).**

Adrian: (▶) *Have you ever been*........ (Have you ever been/Did you ever go) to Churchill, Manitoba?
Josh: Yes. I (1)...went.................... (have gone/went) when I was ten. I remember that I (2).....saw................... (saw/have seen) lots of polar bears there!
Adrian: That sounds exciting! I (3)..have never been (have never been/didn't go) there, but I (4) have heard....... (heard/have heard) many good things about the town from my friends.
Josh: Well, you should travel to Manitoba. There are other places to visit nearby. I remember that I (5)......went.................. (have gone/went) to Wapusk National Park when I was there. It (6)...has been.......... (was/has been) a great experience.

B **Complete the dialogues using the Present Perfect (*I have seen*) or Simple Past (*I saw*).**

A: I (▶) have been.................... (be) looking everywhere for you! Where were you?
B: I (1)..be.......................... (be) at the library in the morning, and I
(2)..have...been........... (be) right here since then.

A: (3)..have...you...seen... (you/see) this movie before?
B: Yes, I (4)....have...seen....... (see) it last week. It's fantastic.

A: Charlie (5)...hfailed.......... (fail) his chemistry test. I can't believe it!
B: I can. He (6)..haven't...opened (not/open) his textbook to study since the first week of school.

A: She (7)..was....been......... (be) painting that room all day, and she's still not finished. Tell her to hurry up.
B: I (8)......te...................... (tell) her, but she can't go any faster.

A: What (9)................................ (do) you do last night?
B: I (10)................................ (go) to a basketball game.

C **Complete this paragraph about the subway system in London, England, by writing the Present Perfect or Simple Past forms of the verbs in parentheses ( ).**

THE LONDON UNDERGROUND

London (▶) has had.............. (have) an underground train system since the ninteenth century. The London Underground (1)..has.....start.. (start) in 1863, when Victorian engineers and workers (2) have....built... (build) the Metropolitan railway. This railway line (3)..has...go......... (go) from Paddington Station to Farringdon Street Station, and steam engines (4) have...pull..... (pull) the coaches. Eleven more lines (5) have open.... (open) since then. The world's first underground electric railway (6)........................ (open) in 1890. This line (7) was....go........ (go) from the City of London to Stockwell in South London. The most modern line is the Jubilee line, which (8) has....open...... (open) in 1979. Since the London Underground (9)..has...begin.. (begin), many other cities, such as New York and Toronto, (10)..have...build. (build) their own systems.

Present Perfect Progressive

1 We form the Present Perfect Progressive like this:

POSITIVE		
	FULL FORM	*SHORT FORM*
I/You/We/They	have been cooking.	've been cooking.
He/She/It	has been cooking.	's been cooking.
NEGATIVE		
I/You/We/They	have not	haven't
He/She/It	has not been cooking.	hasn't been cooking.
QUESTIONS		
Have	I/you/we/they	been cooking?
Has	he/she/it	been cooking?

(For details about **-ing** forms see Appendix 2, page 95.)

2 We use the Present Perfect Progressive for an action or situation that began in the past and continues until now:

*You're late! **I've been waiting** for you.*

We often use **for** and **since** with the Present Perfect Progressive. We use **for** with a period of time, and **since** with a point in time:

*I've been waiting for you **for two hours**.*
*I've been waiting for you **since six o'clock**.*

3 Here are some more examples:

PAST NOW

*Anita **has been talking** on the phone for an hour.* (= She started talking on the phone an hour ago and she is still talking.)
*You've **been sitting** there since one o'clock.* (= You started sitting there at one o'clock and you are still sitting there.)

4 We use the Present Perfect Progressive for actions that are done many times in a period of time from the past until now:

*She's **been taking** driving lessons for a couple of months.* (= She started a couple of months ago; she is still taking lessons.)
*I've **been playing** baseball since I was a small child.*

5 We can use **How long** with the Present Perfect Progressive:

*How long **have** you **been living** here? I **have been living** here for three years.*

Practice

A Complete the sentences by writing the verbs in parentheses ( ) in the Present Perfect Progressive.

► She has been learning........................ (she/learn) Spanish for six months.
1 The roads are very wet; ..has...been....raining.. (it/rain) for hours.
2 we have been playing (we/play) this game for hours. Let's stop now!
3 Wendy has been stadying (Wendy/study) French at school for three years.
4 I has been reading (I/read) this book for months, but I haven't finished it yet.
5 we have been watching (we/watch) this show for hours.
6 have they been making (the neighbours/make) a lot of noise again today?
7 I have been saving.... (I/save) my money for a vacation.
8 .... (you/listen) to me carefully?

B Write *for* or *since* in the blanks.

▶ I've been working in this office since......... last summer.
1 Have you been taking this course ....for...... a long time?
2 I've been driving this car ..since..... more than ten years.
3 She has been planning the party .... the beginning of the month.
4 Nadia has been telling the same stories ....for...... several years.
5 We've been waiting for a reply ..since..... we wrote to them last week.
6 What have you been doing ..since..... the last time that I saw you?
7 You've been writing that email .....for...... more than two hours.
8 He's been feeling sick ...since..... a few days.

C Write sentences to describe what each member of the Lacroix family has been doing to prepare for the holidays. Use words from the box and the Present Perfect Progressive to describe the pictures.

wrap	make
decorate	shop
write	~~put up~~
a cake	cards
~~decorations~~	presents
the tree	for food

▶ Jean has been putting up decorations.
1 Marie and Stephane ..have been making a cake..........
2 Martha ..has been wraping present..........
3 Delia has been decorating the tree..........
4 Tomas ..has been shoping for food..........
5 Crissy ..has been writing cards..........

D Write a sentence for each of the following situations, using the Present Perfect Progressive and *for* or *since*.

▶ She started her course a month ago and she is still taking it.
She has been taking her course for a month.

▶ I started reading this novel last weekend and I'm still reading it.
I have been reading this novel since last weekend.

1 It started snowing at three o'clock and it is still snowing.
it has snowing since three o'clock

2 He started playing chess when he was ten and he still plays it.
he has playing chess since he was ten

3 I started work at eight o'clock and I'm still working.
I have working since eight o'clock

4 Helen started looking for another job two months ago and she's still looking.
helen has looking for another job for two months

5 We arrived here two hours ago and we're still waiting.
we have arriving here for two hours ago

Past Perfect

1 We form the Past Perfect with **had** and the past participle of a verb (e.g. **started, taken**):

	FULL FORM	SHORT FORM
I/You/He/She/It/ We/They	**had started.**	**'d started.**

*I **had taken** it.* OR *I'**d taken** it.*
*They **had not started**.* OR *They **hadn't started**.*

2 Look at this:

A year ago:
Jenny is flying to Rome. She thinks, "I have never been on a plane before now."
Now:
*Jenny flew to Rome last year. She **had** never **been** on a plane before that.*

When we talk about an event or situation in past time we use the Simple Past (e.g. **flew**); if we talk about an event before that time, we use the Past Perfect (e.g. **had been**). Here is another example:

Last Saturday at the theatre:
Mary: *We don't need to line up because I've already bought the tickets.*
Now, talking about last Saturday:
Mary: *We didn't need to line up because I **had** already **bought** the tickets.*

Note that we can use **never** and **already** before the past participle (e.g. **been, bought**).

3 If we talk about a series of past events in order, we use the Simple Past:
A: *I saw a beautiful bird in my backyard.*
B: *I went to get my camera.*
C: *The bird **flew** away.*
D: *I returned with my camera.*

past A B C D (now)

We need the Past Perfect to make it clear that one of the events is not in order:
D: *I returned with my camera.*
C: *The bird **had** already **flown** away.*
(The bird had gone before I returned.)

Also, compare these sentences using **when**:

Simple Past: ***When*** *I returned with my camera, the bird **flew** away.* (It went after I returned.)

Past Perfect: ***When*** *I returned with my camera, the bird **had flown** away.* (It went before I returned.)

4 The Past Perfect is used in reported speech:
*"I have suffered from asthma for many years." She told the doctor that she **had suffered** from asthma for many years.*

(For more on reported speech, see page 56.)

Practice

A **Write sentences about what these people had already done or had never done before. Use the Past Perfect, and *already* or *never*.**

► Yesterday, I had Thai food for the first time.
I had never had Thai food before that.

► Last year, Mohammad ran a marathon for the fourth time.
He had already run three marathons before that.

1 Last week, Francisco wrote an article for the newspaper for the second time.
He had wroted once an article for the newspaper before that.

2 Last month, Adelfina visited Panama for the first time.
She had never visited panama before that.

3 Last year, Junga read *Alice in Wonderland* for the first time.
She had never read Alice in wonderland before that.

4 Last spring, Bruce went camping for the fifth time.
He had went camping before that.

5 Last week, we made ice cream for the third time.
We had made ice cream two time before that.

6 Last month, Gary wore his cowboy boots for the sixth time.
He had wore his cowboy boots for 5 time before that.

B In each case you have two events in the order in which they took place. Write the information in one sentence using the words in parentheses ( ).

► A: The driver started the car. B: Ms. Mangeau appeared.
(When Ms. Mangeau/appear/, the driver/already/start/the car)
When Ms. Mangeau appeared, the driver had already started the car.

1 A: We put the fire out. B: The firefighters arrived.
(When the firefighters/arrive/, we/already/put/the fire out)
when the firefighters arrived, we had already puted the fire...

2 A: Jim finished the work. B: The manager came back.
(When the manager/come/back, Jim/already/finish/the work)
when the manager came back, Jim had already finished the ...

3 A: I went to bed. B: Philip called.
(When Philip/call/, I/already/go/to bed)
when philip called, I had already went to bed

4 A: Alice and Jack had lunch. B: Their children came home.
(When their children/come/home, Alice and Jack/already/have/lunch)
when their children came home, they had already had lunch

5 A: Ian made dinner. B: His wife got home from work.
(When his wife/get/home from work, Ian/already/make/dinner)
when his got home from work, Ian had already made dinner

6 A: The thieves spent the money. B: The police caught them.
(The thieves/already/spend/the money, when the police/catch/them)
....

C Use the Past Perfect to complete the sentences.

► Last summer Pam said, "I've always wanted to fly in a helicopter."
Pam said that she had always wanted to fly in a helicopter.

1 My boss asked me, "Did you file the report?"
My boss asked me if I had did you file report

2 Marcel said, "I saw a fox in the backyard."
Marcel said that he had saw a fox in the backyard

3 Vivienne was talking to Zhi and said, "I enjoyed that hockey game."
Vivienne said that she had enjoyed that hockey game.

4 My dad said, "I've made a batch of cookies."
My dad said that he made a batch of coonies

5 When Dave saw his teacher, he said, "I've finished all my homework."
Dave said that he had finished all my homework.

Will or **be going to**

Compare **will** and **be going to**:

1 We use **will** with an infinitive (**do, go, be, arrive,** etc.):

> INFINITIVE
> *Marcel **will arrive** tomorrow.*

We use **be going** with **to** + infinitive (**to do, to be, to rain,** etc.):

> **to** + INFINITIVE
> *It's **going to snow** soon.*
> *My friends **are going to come** tonight.*
> *It **isn't going to snow** today.*
> *What **are** you **going to do** on Sunday?*

2 We use **will** for actions that we decide to do NOW, at the moment of speaking:

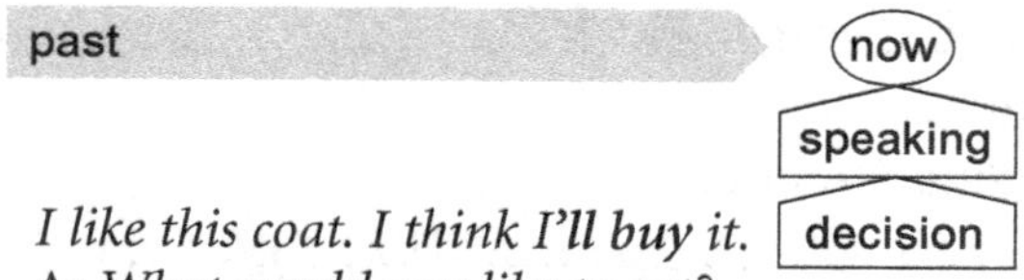

*I like this coat. I think **I'll buy** it.*
A: *What would you like to eat?*
B: ***I'll have** a pizza, please.*

We can use **will** for offers and promises:
*I'**ll carry** your luggage for you.* (OFFER)
*I **won't forget** your birthday again.* (PROMISE)

We use **be going to** for actions that we have decided to do BEFORE we speak:

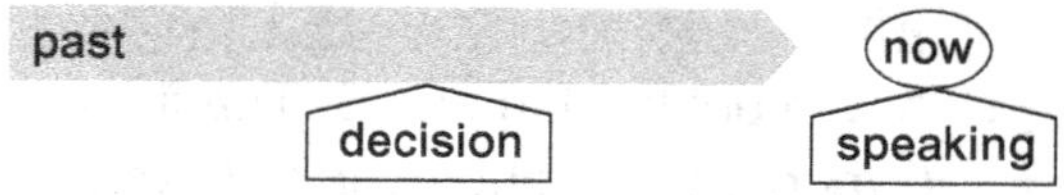

*I'**m going to** clean my room this afternoon.*
(I decided to clean it this morning.)

We can ask questions about people's plans:
***Are** you **going to** take the three o'clock train?*
(= Have you decided to take the three o'clock train?)

3 We use **will** to talk about things that we think or believe will happen in the future:
*I'm sure you'**ll enjoy** the movie.*
*I'm sure it **won't rain** tomorrow. It'**ll be** another beautiful, sunny day.*

We use **be going to** for something that we expect to happen, because the situation now indicates that it is going to happen:
*He's skating towards the goal, and he's **going to** score.*

Practice

A Complete the sentences, using the words in parentheses ( ) and *'ll* or a form of *be going to*.

► A: Are you going to watch TV tonight?
B: Yes, *I'm going to watch* .... (I/watch) my favourite show at nine o'clock.

1 A: Are you going to finish writing your essay tonight?
B: Yes, ... (I/write) it after I watch this movie.

2 A: I'm going to the bookstore. .... (I/buy) that book you want while I'm there.
B: Thanks. .... (I/make) dinner while you're out. But don't be too late; .... (I/meet) Sophie at eight o'clock.

3 A: Are .... (you/compete) in the writing contest this year?
B: .... (I/decide) in a few weeks. If I'm too busy, ... (I/wait) until next year.

4 A: .... (I/wash) my hair before I go out. .... (I/call) you when I'm done.
B: OK. .... (I/be) ready to go when you call.

5 A: Are you planning to go to the party?
B: Yes. .... (I/go) with my brother.

B Look at these office scenes. Choose the correct situation for each scene, then choose the correct sentence and cross out the incorrect one.

▶

....e....

1

....

2

....

3

....

4

....

5

....

a You look hot, I'll open a window./You look hot, I'm going to open a window.

b Next year, we're going to enter the Japanese market./Next year, we'll enter the Japanese market.

c Thanks, I'm going to have an orange juice./Thanks, I'll have an orange juice.

d Take a break. I'm going to do the photocopying./Take a break. I'll do the photocopying.

e Relax, I'll answer it./ ~~Relax, I'm going to answer it.~~

f Thursday is no good for me, I'm afraid. I'll meet the new manager of our Tokyo office./Thursday is no good for me, I'm afraid. I'm going to meet the new manager of our Tokyo office.

C You are at a party. Here are some of the questions you are asked. Reply using *will* or *be going to*.

▶ A: Hi, nice to see you. Would you like a drink?
B: (I/have/a pop, please) I'll have a pop, please...

1 A: Have you seen Gwen lately?
B: (No, but I/see/her next week) ....

2 A: Would you like some appetizers?
B: (Sure, I/have/some shrimp) ....

3 A: Can I give you a tour of the house?
B: (OK, I/follow/you) ....

4 A: Why is everyone going into the living room?
B: (We/sing/karaoke) ....

5 A: Can we meet for lunch tomorrow?
B: (Yes, I/call/you in the morning) ....

Zero Conditional and First Conditional (Real Conditionals)

1 Look at this:

If + SIMPLE PRESENT	+ SIMPLE PRESENT
If I **eat** too much,	I **feel** bad.

(= Every time I eat too much, I feel bad.)

We use this structure (**if + Simple Present + Simple Present**) for facts that are generally true. This structure is called the Zero Conditional:

*If I **don't get** enough sleep, I **feel** tired.*
(= Every time I don't get enough sleep, I feel tired.)
*If you **want** to become a doctor, you **have** to study hard.* (= Anyone who wants to become a doctor has to study hard.)

2 We can say the same thing by reversing the two parts of the sentence:

SIMPLE PRESENT	+ if	+ SIMPLE PRESENT
*I **feel** bad*	***if***	*I **eat** too much.*

Note that we do not use a comma (,) before **if**.

3 Now look at this:

If + SIMPLE PRESENT	+ WILL/WON'T
If I'**m** late,	she'**ll be** angry.

(= Perhaps I will be late; then she'll be angry.)

We use this structure (if + **Simple Present** + **will/won't**) to talk about things that may happen in the future. The verb after **if** is Simple Present, but we use it for a possible future action or situation; we use **will/won't + verb** for the result. This structure is called the First Conditional:

	FUTURE POSSIBILITY	+ RESULT
If	***we don't hurry,***	***we won't finish.***

4 We can reverse the order:
*She'll be angry **if** I'm late.*
*We won't finish **if** we don't hurry.*

5 We do not use **will/won't** after **if**:
NOT ~~If I will be late, she'll be angry.~~

Practice

A Put these facts about various types of people into sentences with *if* + Simple Present + Simple Present. Make *you* the subject of both parts of the sentence.

► Doctors treat people who are sick.
If you're a doctor, you treat people who are sick.

1 Vegetarians don't eat meat.
If you're a vegetarian, ...

2 People who live in a hot country don't like cold weather.
If you live ....

3 Teachers have to work very hard.
If you're a teacher, ...

4 People who do a lot of exercise stay fit and healthy.
If you ....

5 Environmentalists protect the earth.
If you're an ....

6 People who read newspapers know what's happening in the world.
If you ....

B **Complete these sentences with *if* + Simple Present + *will/won't*, using the words in parentheses ( ). Sometimes you do not need to change the words in parentheses.**

► If it snows .... (it/snow), we won't go .... (we/not/go) out.

1 If .... (the weather/be) nice tomorrow, ... (we/drive) to the cottage.

2 If .... (she/mail) the letter now, ... (they/receive) it tomorrow.

3 .... (Fiona/be) angry if .... (John/arrive) late again.

4 .... (I/go) to their party if .... (I/have) enough time.

5 If .... (she/not/pass) this exam, ... (she/not/get) the job that she wants.

6 .... (you/learn) a lot if .... (you/take) this course.

7 If .... (I/get) a ticket, ... (I/go) to the concert.

8 .... (I/buy) that camera if .... (it/not/cost) too much.

9 If .... (you/run) very fast, ... (you/catch) the bus.

10 .... (I/go) to the doctor if .... (I/not/feel) better tomorrow.

11 If .... (they/win) this game, ... (they/be) the champions.

C **Complete the dialogues with the Simple Present or *will/won't* forms of the words in parentheses ( ). Sometimes you do not need to change the words in parentheses.**

► A: We must be at the airport at two o'clock.
B: Well, if we take .... (we/take) a taxi at one o'clock, we won't be .... (we/not/be) late.

1 A: I'd like a bagel.
B: Well, ... (I/buy) one for you if .... (I/go) to the bakery later.

2 A: Has Akiel called yet?
B: No, and if .... (he/not/call) this afternoon, ... (I/call) him this evening.

3 A: Is Jenny there, please?
B: No, but if .... (you/want) to leave a message, ... (I/give) it to her.

4 A: Is Will going to pass his test?
B: Well, ... (he/fail) if .... (he/not/work) harder.

5 A: Could I have some information about this year's concerts, please?
B: Yes, if .... (you/fill in) this form, ... (I/send) the information to your email account.

Present tense: **when**, **before**, **after**, **until**, etc.

1 Look at this sentence:

When the show ends, I'll do the dishes.

To talk about an event in the future, we usually use the Simple Present (e.g. **ends**) after **when, before, after, until,** and **as soon as**. We do not use **will**:

*I'm going to finish this work **before I go**.*
(NOT ... ~~*before I will go.*~~)
*Wait here **until I get** back.*
*I'll call you **as soon as I arrive**.*

2 We can use **when** + Simple Present to refer to a time when something will happen:

*I'll buy some ice cream **when I'm** at the store.*

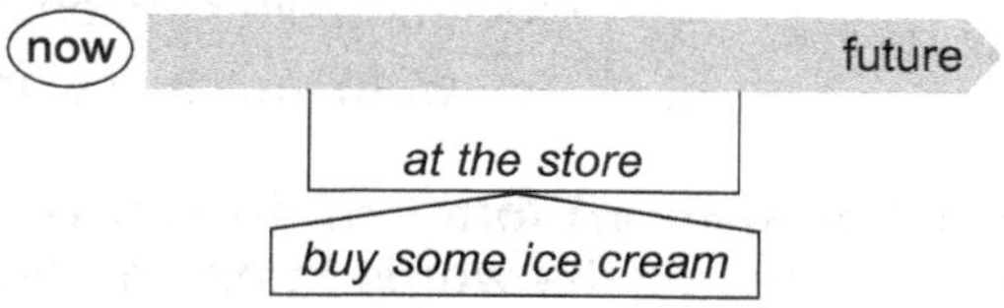

***When** you **see** her, give her my message.*

We use **until** + Present Simple to mean from now to a time in the future:

*We'll sit outside **until** it **gets** dark.* (= We'll sit outside from now to when it gets dark.)

We use **as soon as** + Simple Present with the meaning "immediately after":

*They'll start playing **as soon as it stops** raining.* (= They will start playing immediately after the rain stops.)

3 We use **when** + Present Perfect (e.g. **I have done**) to talk about an action that must, or will, happen before the next action can happen:

***When I've found** a job, I'll look for a place to live.* (= First I will find a job; then I will look for a place to live.)

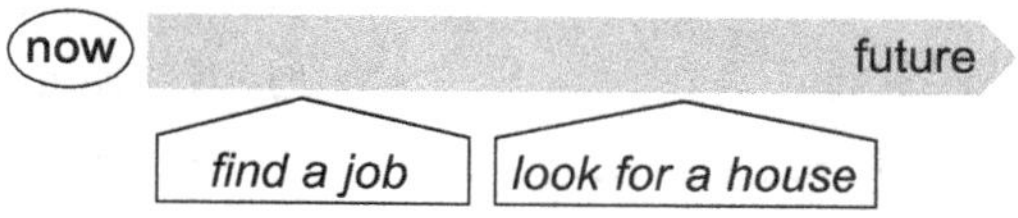

***When** Simon **has saved** enough money, he'll buy a car.* (= First Simon must save the money; then he can buy a car.)

4 With **after** we can use either the Simple Present or the Present Perfect with no difference in meaning:

*After she **takes/has taken** the program, she'll be a qualified teacher.* (= When she has finished her program, she'll be a qualified teacher.)

Practice

A **Complete the sentences by writing *when*, *before*, *after*, *as soon as*, or *until* in the blanks. Sometimes more than one answer is possible.**

► I'll stay in this job until.......... I find a better one.
1 I'm going to keep working .... I finish this.
2 Remember to buy some stamps .... you're at the post office.
3 .... I speak to him on the phone tonight, I'll ask him.
4 We can go for a dinner .... we've seen the movie.
5 I'll keep looking for it .... I find it.
6 I'll wait for them .... it gets dark, and then I'll leave.
7 Don't forget to lock the door .... you go out.
8 .... I've found the information, I'll call you.
9 We'll wait .... it stops snowing, and then we'll go out.
10 .... you see Murad, tell him I said hi.
11 Submit your application .... the deadline.
12 You shouldn't wait. You should reply .... you receive the invitation.
13 Book a table .... you go to the restaurant. It's often full.

B **Complete the dialogues, using the Simple Present or *will* forms of the verbs in parentheses ( ). Sometimes you do not need to change the word in parentheses.**

► A: Could you pick up some new socks for me, please?
B: Yes, I'll do......... (do) it when I go............ (go) to the mall.

1 A: I might be late tonight.
B: OK. I .... (wait) until you .... (arrive).

2 A: I'm leaving next week.
B: I .... (see) you before you .... (go), won't I?

3 A: Have you decided what you're going to do on the weekend yet?
B: No, but I .... (call) you as soon as I .... (know) what I'm going to do.

4 A: Have you done that homework yet?
B: No, not yet. I .... (do) it when I .... (have) enough time.

5 A: I don't want to go to that party tonight.
B: Well, I'm sure you .... (enjoy) it when you .... (get) there.

6 A: Could you tell Carlos to call me, please?
B: Yes, I .... (tell) him when I .... (see) him tomorrow.

7 A: Mr Jackson isn't in at the moment.
B: I see. Well, I .... (wait) until he .... (come) back.

8 A: Have you booked a hotel in Niagara Falls yet?
B: No, but we .... (book) one before we .... (go) there.

9 A: Don't forget to email Josh.
B: OK. I .... (do) it as soon as I .... (get) home.

10 A: .... (you/see) Jack when you .... (be) in St. John's?
B: Yes, I hope I will. I .... (phone) him when I .... (arrive) in Newfoundland.

C **Complete the sentences using the Present Perfect or *will* forms of the verbs in parentheses ( ).**

► When you have written...... (write) that letter, I'll mail....... (mail) it for you.

1 I .... (pay) the bill when I have borrowed some money from somebody.
2 When I've found a car that I want to buy, I .... (ask) my bank to lend me the money to buy it.
3 After the plane .... (land), you may unfasten your seat belts.
4 When you .... (check) all your answers, hand in your test.
5 I .... (read) this book when I'm on vacation.
6 When I .... (read) this magazine, I'll start work.
7 You .... (feel) better when you have had something to eat.
8 When you .... (finish) your work, you can go home.
9 She .... (be) pleased when she hears the news.
10 Let's go for a walk after we .... (have) dinner.

So am I, I am too, Neither am I, etc.

1 Look at this:

She is saying that she is also tired.

2 Here are some more examples:

*He **was** very angry. ~ So **was** I.*

*My apartment is small. ~ So **is mine**.*
*They **were** waiting. ~ So **was she**.*
*I**'m** going to have some pop. ~ So **am** I.*
*Ann **has** finished her work and so **has** Mary.*
*They**'ve** been waiting. ~ So **has** she.*
*I **work** in an office. ~ So **do** I.*
*I **enjoyed** the movie. ~ So **did** I.*
*Dan **will** pass the exam and so **will** you.*
*He **can** drive. ~ So **can** she.*

Note:
- we use **so** after a positive statement;
- the verb we use after **so** depends on the verb used in the positive statement.

3 Instead of **so am I**, we can say **I am too**, with the same meaning. Here are some examples:

*I'm tired.~ **I am too.***
*We've got a small apartment. ~ **We do too.***
*I work in an office. ~ **I do too.***
*Bill enjoyed the movie and **I did too.***
*He can drive. ~ **She can too.***

4 We can use expressions like **neither am I** to reply to a negative statement:

*I'm not tired. ~ Neither **am** I.*
(= And I'm not tired.)
*I haven't seen that movie. ~ Neither **have** I.*
*I don't like this place. ~ Neither **do** I.*
*I didn't see that play. ~ Neither **did** I.*
*His sister can't drive and neither **can he**.*

5 We can say **I'm not either** to mean the same as **neither am I**:

*I'm not tired. ~ **I'm not** either.*
(= And I'm not tired.)
*I haven't seen that movie. ~ **I haven't** either.*
*I don't like this place. ~ **I don't** either.*
*I didn't see that play. ~ **I didn't** either.*
*His sister can't drive and **he can't** either.*

Practice

A Complete the sentences with *so*, *too*, *either*, or *neither*.

- I really enjoyed that meal. ~ So............ did I.
- I haven't done the homework. ~ I haven't either......... .
- We live downtown. ~ We do too............ .

1 I don't like football. ~ .... do I.
2 I haven't been to New York. ~ .... have I.
3 My father works in an office. ~ .... does mine.
4 I haven't read a newspaper today. ~ .... have I.
5 I play a lot of different sports. ~ I do ....
6 I've been working very hard lately. ~ .... have I.
7 Ann will be at the party and .... will Jaclyn.
8 My brother can't speak any foreign languages and .... can my sister.
9 Helen sent me a birthday card and Robin did ....
10 Jorge isn't going to the meeting and I'm not ....
11 Tony arrived late and .... did I.
12 Mia didn't go to the concert and .... did I.

B **Write the replies, using *so* or *neither* and the words in parentheses ( ), as in the examples.**

QUESTIONS	ANSWERS
► I've got a cold. (I)	So do I.
► I don't have much money. (I)	Neither do I.
1 We're going to the concert. (we)	....
2 My pen doesn't work. (mine)	....
3 I haven't read today's paper. (I)	....
4 My meal was excellent. (mine)	....
5 I've been sick. (Frank)	....
6 Ron didn't go to the party. (George)	....
7 I can't understand this game. (I)	....
8 I'm not working tomorrow. (I)	....
9 Ruth passed the exam. (Lannie)	....
10 I've eaten enough. (I)	....
11 I'm going to see that movie. (we)	....
12 My car is very old. (mine)	....

C **Look at the information in the table about four people and complete the sentences using *so*, *too*, *either*, or *neither*.**

	JULIA	ROBERT	SANDRA	PAUL
Lives in:	Toronto	Montreal	Toronto	Halifax
Speaks:	Spanish	French	Spanish	French
Drives?	Yes	No	No	Yes
Likes:	reading	travelling	travelling	reading
Plays:	basketball	basketball	hockey	hockey

► Julia lives in Toronto and Sandra does too........ .

► Julia lives in Toronto and so does............. Sandra.

1 Robert doesn't live in Toronto and .... Paul.

2 Robert doesn't live in Toronto and Paul ....

3 Julia speaks Spanish and .... Sandra.

4 Julia speaks Spanish and Sandra ....

5 Robert can't speak Spanish and .... Paul.

6 Robert can't speak Spanish and Paul ....

7 Julia can drive and Paul ....

8 Robert can't drive and .... Sandra.

9 Julia has passed her driving test and .... Paul.

10 Robert likes travelling and .... Sandra.

11 Julia likes reading and Paul ....

12 Julia plays basketball and .... Robert.

13 Sandra doesn't play basketball and .... Paul.

Verb + preposition

1 After some verbs we use a particular preposition* (e.g. **for, to, on**):

VERB + PREPOSITION	
wait for:	*I was **waiting for** a bus.*
listen to:	*She **listens to** the radio a lot.*
belong to:	*Does that book **belong to** you?*
ask for:	*Have you **asked for** the bill?*
apply for:	*He has **applied for** another job.*
depend on:	*The salary **depends on** your education.*
agree with:	*I don't **agree with** you.*

2 Now look at these examples:

- **arrive at/in:**
  *We **arrived at the airport**.* (You **arrive at** a place, for example a building.)
  *We **arrived in Portugal**.* (You **arrive in** a town or country.)
- **look at/for:**
  ***Look at** that strange **sculpture** over there!* (You **look at** something you can see.)
  *I'm **looking for** my **mittens**.* (You **look for** something that you are trying to find.)
- **talk to/about:**
  *She was **talking to** some friends.* (You **talk to** somebody.)
  *They were **talking about** politics.* (You **talk about** something.)

3 In questions that begin with a question word like **What, Who,** or **How many,** we usually put the preposition at the end:
Who are you waiting for?
Who does this jacket belong to?

4 We do not usually use a preposition after these verbs:

call (on the phone): *He **called** me last night.* (NOT ~~*He called to me*~~ ...)
discuss: *We often **discuss** hockey.* (NOT ... ~~*discuss about hockey*~~.)
answer: *She didn't **answer** me.* (NOT ... ~~*answer to me*~~.)
reach (= arrive): *I **reached** the office at nine o'clock.* (NOT ... ~~*reached to the office*~~ ...)

5 Note that we **pay someone**, but we **pay for something:**
*She paid **him** yesterday.* (You **pay** a person.)
*I paid **for** the books.* (You **pay for** something that you receive.)

But note that we **pay** a bill: *I'll **pay** the bill.*

*Another term for **verb + preposition** is **prepositional verb.**

Practice

A Complete these sentences with the correct prepositions (*to*, *for*, etc.). In some sentences no preposition is required.

- ► I'm waiting for............ a telephone call.
- ► We reached –.............. the airport after eleven o'clock.

1 I'll ask .... some information.
2 Let's listen .... some music.
3 Where do I pay .... this shirt?
4 Let's discuss .... the plans for tomorrow.
5 Who's going to pay .... the taxi driver?
6 We paid .... the bill and left the restaurant.
7 I'll call .... the theatre and buy two tickets.
8 The price of the vacation depends .... when you want to travel.
9 He walked out of the room without answering .... me.
10 A lot of people don't agree .... you.
11 I've applied .... a visa.
12 Who does this pen belong .... ?

B **Complete the story by writing a preposition in the blank if one is necessary. For some blanks, no preposition is required.**

When Jack arrived (▶) at............ the bar, Alice was waiting (1)................ him. "Where have you been?" she asked (2)................ him. "We can talk (3)................ that later," said Jack. "I tried to call (4)................ you to say that I was going to be late, but your phone was turned off. Let's go to the concert." "OK," said Alice, "but since you were late, you have to pay (5)................ the tickets!" "What?" said Jack. "I don't want to argue (6)................ it, but I don't agree (7)................ you. It's not fair!"

C **Complete the questions using the words in parentheses ( ). Add the correct preposition, if any.**

Gajendra: What are you doing here, Pam?
Pam: I'm just waiting.
Gajendra: (who/you/wait) (▶) Who are you waiting for?...........................
Pam: Sara. She's talking to the boss.
Gajendra: (what/they/talk) (1)..
Pam: She wants more money.
Gajendra: (how much/she/ask) (2)..
Pam: I don't know, but she's thinking about looking for a new job.
Gajendra: (how many jobs/have/she/apply) (3)..
Pam: Five or six, I think. By the way, is that a new book that you've got?
Gajendra: It's new but it's not mine.
Pam: And (what/you/read) (4)..
Gajendra: The new Rohinton Mistry novel. It's great!

D **Complete the postcard by writing in the prepositions that are necessary. Sometimes, no preposition is required.**

Dear Sam,

We arrived (▶) in.............. Greece at about eleven o'clock. We got a taxi from the airport to the port, and then we took a lovely little boat to the island. I enjoyed looking (1)................ the scenery on the way. When we reached (2)................ the island, we looked (3)................ our villa but we couldn't find it. I talked (4)................ a local man, and I asked (5)................ directions. He offered to take me there. When we arrived (6)................ the villa, I offered to pay (7)................ him, but he didn't want any money. The weather's lovely. I'll call (8)................ you when we get back from our vacation.

Love,

Tina

Make, do, have, get

1 There are many phrases in which a particular verb is used together with a particular noun, for example:
*make a cup of **coffee***
*do some **work***
*have **breakfast***

2 We often use **make** in sentences about producing or creating something:
*They **made a fire** in the woods.*
*Shall I **make** some **coffee**?*
*He **made** some **sandwiches** for lunch.*

3 We also use **make** in these phrases:
*Excuse me. I have to **make a phone call**.*
*He **makes** a lot of **mistakes** in his work.*
*I couldn't sleep because the neighbours were **making** a lot of **noise**.*
*You should **make** your **bed** in the morning.*

4 We often use **do** in sentences about working, or about particular jobs:
*Have you **done** your **homework**?*
*He offered to **do the dishes**.*
*We're going to **do** some **shopping**.*
*I haven't **done** much **work** today.*

5 We use **have** + **noun** to describe activities:
*We usually **have lunch** at about one o'clock.*
*I'm **having fish** for dinner tonight.*
*I **had a nap** in the park this afternoon.*

6 We use **get** with adjectives that describe feelings, to say that we begin to have the feeling:
*I'm **getting tired** now. I need a break.*
*They're late and I'm **getting worried**.*
*I **got angry** and shouted at them.*

7 We use **get** in some phrases that describe a change of situation:
*We **got lost** in Toronto.* (= We became lost ...)
*It's **getting cold**.* (= It's becoming cold.)
*Jane was very sick, but she's **getting better**.*
*They **got married** three years ago.*
*It rained heavily and I **got** very **wet**.*

8 We use **make** + **someone** + **adjective** to talk about the cause of a feeling:
*He **made us** very **angry**.*
*The news **made him happy**.*

Practice

A Complete the sentences, using the correct forms of *make*, *do*, *have*, or *get*. Be careful that you use the correct tense.

► He was ~~making~~....... a cup of coffee in the kitchen.
► We ~~had~~........... lunch in a very nice little restaurant yesterday.
1 We don't have any maple syrup. I'll have to .... some from the store.
2 Can we .... plans to do something on Saturday?
3 Do you .... some time to talk about this problem?
4 When she was younger, she .... a dog named George.
5 We really should go for a jog. We haven't .... anything all day.
6 How will you .... to Iqaluit? No roads go all the way there.
7 When should we .... dinner?
8 The car is stuck again. I'll .... the shovel.
9 Please .... a pot of coffee.
10 Have you .... the laundry yet?
11 I wasn't familiar with the city, so I .... lost.
12 I've never .... Indian food before. Is it good?

B **Look at the notes in the box about what Laura did yesterday. Complete the sentences, using the correct forms of *make*, *do*, *have*, or *get*. Sometimes more than one answer is possible.**

7:30	Got up. Bed.
8:00	Breakfast (orange juice and toast).
8:30–9:00	Walk to work. Rain.
9:00–1:00	Work. Very busy.
1:00–2:00	Lunch in office. Sandwiches.
2:00–5:00	Work. Finished everything.
5:30	Shopping. Home.
7:00	Pizza for dinner. Dishes.
8:00–11:00	TV. Tired. Bed.

It was a normal day for Laura yesterday. She got up at seven-thirty and she (►) made......... the bed. Then she (1)................ breakfast. For breakfast she (2)................ orange juice and toast. While she was walking to work, it rained and she (3)................ wet. She (4)................ angry about this. In the morning she (5)................ a lot of work. She (6)................ lunch at about one o'clock. She (7)................ sandwiches for lunch. When she had (8)................ all her work in the afternoon, she went home. On the way home she (9)................ some shopping. She (10)................ a pizza for dinner. She (11)................ the dishes and then she watched TV for three hours. By eleven o'clock she felt tired, and so she went to bed.

C **Complete the dialogues, using the correct form of *make*, *do*, *have*, or *get*.**

► A: Was the movie good?
B: No, I got........... bored in the middle of it.

1 A: Dinner's ready!
B: It smells delicious. What did you .... ?

2 A: Do you .... any allergies?
B: Yes, I'm allergic to peanuts.

3 A: I can't reach the jar on the top shelf.
B: I'll .... it down for you.

4 A: What do you have in that bag?
B: It's a book that I .... from my sister.

5 A: Have you already booked our plane tickets?
B: No, Jen is .... the reservation right now.

6 A: The bathroom is flooding! What should we .... ?
B: Call a plumber.

7 A: Why weren't you at work yesterday?
B: I .... the flu.

Word order: subject, verb, object

1 In English, the order of words in a statement is subject + verb + object:

SUBJECT +	VERB	+ OBJECT
I	*enjoy*	*good food.*
Peter	*is watching*	*TV.*
She	*drank*	*a cup of coffee.*

2 Some verbs (e.g. **go**) do not have an object:
Steven ***has gone.***
The train ***didn't arrive.***
Ann and Tom ***are swimming.***

Some verbs (e.g. **like**) always need an object:

SUBJECT +	VERB	+ OBJECT
I	*like*	*music.*
She	*wants*	*a drink.*

3 After the verb **be**, we can use an object or an adjective:

	OBJECT
She is	*a doctor.*

	ADJECTIVE
Mary is	*tired.*

We can also put adjectives after the verbs **look, seem,** and **feel:**
Mary ***looks tired.***

4 Now look at this example:

John gave ***Mary*** *an apple.*
John gave ***her*** *an apple.*

After some verbs (e.g. **give, send, bring**), we can talk about a person (**Mary, her**) and an object:

	VERB	+ PERSON +	OBJECT
He	*sent*	*Jane*	*a book.*
Ann	*made*	*Tom*	*a cup of tea.*
Ann	*brought*	*him*	*a cup of tea.*
He	*left*	*them*	*some money.*
She	*wrote*	*him*	*a letter.*

5 We usually put information about times or places at the end of the sentence:

	PLACE
I took a vacation	*in Panama.*

	TIME
They gave their son a watch	*yesterday.*

Practice

A There are ten sentences in the box. Circle each sentence.

Jack hit the ball they play hockey we've eaten dinner Samantha married Michael Janice wrote a book I don't want to go she is a doctor the car is blue no one's happy the kids saw a movie

B Write the words in parentheses ( ) in the correct order.

► (bought – she – a TV) She bought a TV.
1 (she – a book – is reading) ....
2 (caught – he – a fish) ....
3 (to Paris – have been – we) ....
4 (me – bit – the dog) ....
5 (Emma – to dance – likes) ....
6 (ate – a hamburger – Mark) ....
7 (to school – is walking – Sam) ....

8 (are learning – they – English) ....

9 (them – are teaching – the girls) ....

10 (played – guitar – Sarah) ....

11 (we – a vacation – want) ....

12 (tired – the kids – are) ....

C If the words are in the correct order, put a check (✓). If not, write the correct sentence.

► Mary has cooked. ✓..

► Fantastic was the movie. The movie was fantastic.

1 Home we drove after school together. ....

2 We share did not the sandwich. ....

3 Jim has played lacrosse for many years. ....

4 Marie is having not fun. ....

5 They are tired and hungry. ....

D Write sentences, putting the word in parentheses ( ) in the correct place.

► She wrote a letter. (me) She wrote me a letter.

1 Her dad bought a new car. (her) ....

2 I made a cup of tea. (you) ....

3 Vish baked cookies yesterday. (his grandma) ....

4 Everyone is sending a birthday card. (Daryl) ....

5 The class is buying a present. (the teacher) ....

6 Janice gave a treat. (the dog) ....

7 She is not leaving a note. (her husband) ....

8 Khalida is writing an email. (her sister) ....

E Write the word in parentheses ( ) in the correct place in the sentence.

► (bought) We bought....... a house .... in Italy ....

1 (football) Justin .... doesn't play .... anymore.

2 (is visiting) Max .... Paris .... next summer.

3 (you) I .... sent .... flowers .... on your birthday.

4 (a letter) David .... wrote .... Sonya .... yesterday.

5 (excellent). The book .... was ....

6 (last month). My parents .... took .... a vacation ....

7 (is buying) She .... her friend .... a gift.

8 (me) Sue .... told .... a beautiful story.

9 (that book) I .... read .... quickly ....

10 (Spanish) Both my brothers .... are studying .... at school ....

11 (made) My mom .... chicken soup .... for me .... when I was sick.

12 (was) Nicole .... excited .... about the trip.

13 (you) I .... mailed .... a letter .... yesterday.

14 (hungry) The boys .... are ....

Who and **what**: subject and object

1 Compare these examples:

	SUBJECT	
Ann:	*Who*	***told** you?*
Mary:	*Gino told me.*	

This is a subject question.

	OBJECT	
Ann:	*Who*	***did** you **tell**?*
Mary:	*I told Bill.*	

This is an object question.

2 Compare subject and object questions with **who**:

In the sentence *Who told you?* **Who** is the subject. Here is another example:

Ann: SUBJECT *Who* ***wrote** Hamlet?*
(= **Somebody** wrote Hamlet. Who?)
Mary: *Shakespeare wrote Hamlet.*

When **who** is the subject, the order of the words is the same as in a statement:

SUBJECT	
Who	***is going** to go with me?*
Who	***lives** in that old house?*
Who	***wants** some more coffee?*

In the sentence *Who did you tell?* **Who** is the object. Here is another example:

Ann: OBJECT *Who* ***did** you **meet** last night?*
(= You met **somebody**. Who?)
Mary: *I met a couple of friends.*

When **who** is the object, we use an auxiliary (**be**, **do**, **have**, etc.) before the subject:

OBJECT	
Who	***are** you **going** to invite?*
Who	***did** Laura **ask** for help?*
Who	***have** you **told** about this?*

3 Compare subject and object questions with **what**:

SUBJECT	
What	***is** in this dish?*

(= **Something** is in it. What?)

OBJECT	
What	***did** you **buy** at the store?*

(= You bought **something**. What?)

Practice

A Use the sentences in parentheses ( ) to write questions beginning with *Who* or *What*.

- ► (Eric met **somebody**.) *Who did Eric meet?*
- ► (**Somebody** ate the last piece of pizza.) *Who ate the last piece of pizza?*
1. (**Somebody** wants some more coffee.) ....
2. (**Something** happened at the end of the story.) ....
3. (**Somebody** is going to pay the bill.) ....
4. (He had **something** for breakfast.) ....
5. (Their letter said **something**.) ....
6. (**Somebody** knows the answer to my question.) ....
7. (They saw **something**.) ....
8. (She is calling **somebody**.) ....

B **Use the full answers to write questions using *Who* or *What*. (We usually use the short, underlined answers when we reply to a question.)**

QUESTIONS	ANSWERS
► Who were you talking to on the phone ?	~ (I was talking to) Elizabeth (on the phone).
► What was the final score ?	~ (The final score was) 2–0 for the Flames.
1 .... ?	~ Anita and Frank (went on the trip).
2 .... ?	~ I'm not sure (what's happening in this movie).
3 .... ?	~ (I'm going to call) Jeff.
4 .... ?	~ (I watched) that new series (on TV last night).
5 .... ?	~ John (sent these flowers).
6 .... ?	~ (I bought) a book (in that store).
7 .... ?	~ Some good news (has made Ray so happy).

C **Read this story and then complete the questions.**

Two days ago Robert took his driving test. He failed it. Afterwards he met his friend Philip. He told Philip that he had failed his test. Then he said, "Don't tell anyone. It's a secret." Philip said, "OK, I won't tell anyone." Later that day, Philip met Linda for coffee and he said, "Robert failed his driving test." Linda laughed. "Poor Robert," she said.

QUESTIONS	ANSWERS
► (What/Robert/do/two days ago?) What did Robert do two days ago?	~ He took his driving test.
1 (What/happen?)	~ He failed it.
2 (Who/take/his/driving test?)	~ Robert.
3 (What/Robert/fail?)	~ His driving test.
4 (What/Robert/say/to Philip?)	~ He said, "Don't tell anyone."
5 (Who/meet/Linda/for coffee?)	~ Philip.

D **Complete the questions for the following answers. Use the words in parentheses ( ).**

► (Oswald, kill) Who did Oswald kill ?	~ He killed President Kennedy.
► (Kennedy, kill) Who killed Kennedy ?	~ Oswald killed Kennedy.
1 (the Nobel Prize, win) Who .... for Physics in 1909?	~ Marconi.
2 (Bell, invent) What .... ?	~ Telephone.
3 (Everest, climb) Who .... with Hillary?	~ Sherpa Tenzing.
4 (Prince William, marry) Who .... ?	~ He married Kate.
5 (Hiroshima, destroy) What .... ?	~ An atomic bomb.
6 (Gretzky, play) What .... ?	~ Hockey.

How long/far/often ...?

1 We use **How long ...?** to ask about a period of time:

How long have you been waiting? ~ About twenty minutes.
How long will the trip take? ~ Three hours.

We use **from ... to** or **from ... until** to talk about a period of time:

*She was a student **from** 2009 **to** 2012.*
*Tomorrow I'm working **from** 8:30 **until** 6.*

2 We use **How far ...?** to ask about the distance from one place to another. We can use **from** and **to** with the places we are asking about:

*How far is it **from** Regina **to** Saskatoon? ~ 260 kilometres.*
*How far is your cottage **from** here? ~ Not far.*

3 We use **How often ...?** to ask about the number of times something happens. We can use phrases like **every day, once a week,** etc. in the answer:

*How often do the buses run? ~ **Every hour.***
*How often do you play lacrosse? ~ **Twice a week.***

4 We can use **How much ...?** to ask about the price of something:

How much is a round-trip to Vancouver?
How much did you pay for this car?

5 We use **How much ...?** with an uncountable noun to ask about the amount of something. An uncountable noun cannot be plural because it describes something that cannot be counted (e.g. **bread, work, weather, money, music, meat, milk, cheese**).

How much bread is there in the kitchen?
How much work have you done today?

6 We use **How many ...?** with a plural noun to ask about numbers:

How many students are in your class? ~ Fifteen.
How many people went to the party? ~ Ten.

7 We use **How old ...?** to ask about someone's age:

How old are you? ~ I'm 19.

Note that we say:

I am 19, OR: *19.* (NOT ~~*I have 19.*~~)

We can also say: *I'm 19 years old.* But we cannot say: ~~*I'm 19 years.*~~

Practice

A Complete the questions using *How long*, *How old*, *How often*, etc. Change the verbs into the correct tense.

QUESTIONS / ANSWERS

► (How/you/stay/in New Zealand?)
How long did you stay in New Zealand? ~ I stayed there for six months.

1 (How/he/read/a newspaper?)
.... ~ He reads one every day.

2 (How/a single room/cost?)
.... ~ It costs $100 a night.

3 (How/be/you when you went to live in Montreal?)
.... ~ I was 15 when I went there.

4 (How/courses/you/going to take?)
.... ~ I'm going to take three courses.

5 (How/the course/last?)
.... ~ It will last for two years.

6 (How/be/it from here to the nearest bus stop?)
.... ~ It's about 200 metres.

B **Write each question using the words in parentheses ( ), and *How old*, *How much*, *How many*, etc. Change the verbs into the correct tense.**

► A: How old is your husband .... (your husband/be)?
B: He is 34. He'll be 35 next month.

1 A: .... (languages/you/speak)?
B: I speak three – English, French, and Chinese.

2 A: .... (it/be) from here to the airport?
B: It's about 25 kilometres.

3 A: .... (the meal/cost)?
B: I can't remember, but it wasn't very expensive.

4 A: .... (you/stay) there?
B: I stayed there from June until October.

5 A: .... (the delivery man/come)?
B: He comes twice a day.

6 A: .... (cheese/you/buy)?
B: I bought half a kilogram.

C **Complete each of these sentences by writing one word in each blank.**

► It was my birthday last week. I am............ 21.

1 The show lasts .... eight-thirty .... ten o'clock.
2 There is a train to Union Station .... 30 minutes in the morning.
3 How .... money have you got?
4 How far is it .... here .... Robson Street?
5 My grandfather is 70 ....
6 How .... countries have you visited?

D **Complete the conversation by writing Bob's questions. Start with *How* ... each time.**

Anne: I'm taking a course in accounting.
Bob: Oh really? (►) How long have you been taking it?..
Anne: I've been taking it for about a month. It's at the local college.
Bob: (1)...?
Anne: I go there twice a week.
Bob: (2)...?
Anne: The classes last for three hours, from two o'clock until five.
Bob: (3)...?
Anne: I study at home every evening.
Bob: (4)...?
Anne: There are about 25 people in my class.
Bob: (5)...?
Anne: They're all about the same age as me.
Bob: (6)...?
Anne: It's not far from my home.
Bob: (7)...?
Anne: It doesn't cost anything. My company is paying.

Question tags

1 A question tag is a short question (e.g. **isn't it?**, **haven't we?**) that we can add at the end of a statement:
Vytas: *We've met before, **haven't we?***
Terry: *Yes, we have.*

2 Look at this part of a conversation:
Breanne: *Sandra is Swiss.*
Sioban: *No, she's French, **isn't she?***
(= I thought she was French, but am I wrong?)

When tag questions really are questions, like Sioban's, the voice goes up at the end.

But when tag questions are not really questions, the voice goes down at the end:

*That was a boring play, **wasn't it?***
(= I think that was a boring play.)

3 Note that the verb we use in the tag depends on the verb used in the statement:

	VERB	+ TAG
be:	*You're French,*	*aren't you?*
verb:	*He plays golf,*	*doesn't he?*
auxiliary verb:	*It has arrived,*	*hasn't it?*

Thus, most verbs use **do/does**, while **be** and **auxiliary verbs** use the same verb in the question tag.

4 A positive statement has a negative tag:

POSITIVE	+ NEGATIVE
I'm right,	***aren't I?*** (NOT ~~*am't I?*~~)
You're 18,	***aren't you?***
They're getting tired,	***aren't they?***
They were friendly,	***weren't they?***
He lives in Gatineau	***doesn't he?***
You speak Spanish,	***don't you?***
You passed your test,	***didn't you?***
She has left,	***hasn't she?***
You can drive,	***can't you?***
The bus will come soon,	***won't it?***

5 A negative statement has a positive tag:

NEGATIVE	+ POSITIVE
It isn't very cheap,	***is it?***
We aren't going to be late,	***are we?***
She wasn't angry,	***was she?***
You don't like this,	***do you?***
She didn't win,	***did she?***
She hasn't visited Mexico,	***has she?***
She can't drive,	***can she?***
It won't snow today,	***will it?***

Practice

A Complete the conversation by writing question tags.

Lee: We haven't met before, (▶) have we ?
Sarah: No, I've just arrived in this country.
Lee: You come from Australia, (1)........................ ?
Sarah: Yes, from Sydney.
Lee: It's very hot there, (2)........................ ?
Sarah: Most of the time, but not always.
Lee: But it never gets very cold, (3)........................ ?
Sarah: No, well, not as cold as some places.
Lee: They speak English there, (4)........................ ?
Sarah: Yes, that's right.
Lee: You haven't been here long, (5)........................ ?
Sarah: No, I only got here two weeks ago.
Lee: You're on vacation, (6)........................ ?
Sarah: Yes, I'm travelling around Canada for six months.

B Complete the sentences by writing question tags.

► The movie starts at seven o'clock, doesn't it.......... ? ~ Yes, that's right.
1 I can use this ticket on any bus, ... ? ~ Yes, you can.
2 The bill won't be very high, ... ? ~ No, I don't think so.
3 He wasn't very polite, ... ? ~ No, he wasn't.
4 I didn't make a mistake, ... ? ~ No, you didn't.
5 It won't be a difficult thing to do, ... ? ~ No, I don't think so.
6 That was a lovely meal, ... ? ~ Yes, it was delicious.
7 You can't play the piano, ... ? ~ No, I can't.
8 They left last week, ... ? ~ Yes, that's right.

C Complete the conversation with question tags.

Charles: You're going to Iqaluit this week, (►) aren't you.......... ?
Marta: Yes, I'm going tomorrow.
Charles: Iqaluit is in Nunavut, (1)........................ ?
Marta: Yes, it's the capital.
Charles: You've been there before, (2)........................ ?
Marta: Yes, two years ago.
Charles: But you can't speak Inuktitut, (3)........................ ?
Marta: No, I can't.
Charles: But most people from Iqaluit speak English, (4)........................ ?
Marta: Yes.
Charles: Well, I'll see you before you leave, (5)........................ ?
Marta: Yes, I'll see you tonight.

D Complete each sentence with a question tag before the reply.

► A: She comes from Italy, doesn't she?..
B: Yes, she comes from Italy.
1 A: You can ....
B: Yes, I can speak French very well.
2 A: You haven't ....
B: No, I haven't heard this story.
3 A: You went ....
B: Yes, I went to Frank's party.
4 A: It isn't ....
B: No, it isn't very far from here.
5 A: She won't ....
B: No, she won't be angry.
6 A: You're not ....
B: No, I'm not going to leave now.
7 A: You'll ....
B: Yes, I'll be at home tonight.

Must, must not

1 We use **must** with an infinitive (**do**, **go**, **work**, etc.):

		INFINITIVE	
You	***must***	***work***	*harder.*

Don't use **to** before the infinitive:
NOT ~~*You must to work harder.*~~

The form of **must** is the same for all persons:

I/You/He/She/It/We/They **must leave** soon.

2 We use **must** in rules, to say that an action is necessary:
*All visitors **must go** to reception when they arrive.*

We use **You must ...** to give somebody an order:
*Your work is poor – **you must try** harder.*
***You must finish** this work tomorrow.*

We use **I/We must ...** to say that we think it is necessary or important that we do something:
*I'm getting tired. **I must go** home now.*
***We must get** a new car soon.*

3 We also use **You must ...** to strongly recommend or offer something:
***You must read** this book; it's fantastic!*
***You must come** for lunch at our house.*

4 The negative form of **must** is **must not** (occasionally ***mustn't***):
*You **must not park** here – it's not allowed.*
NOT ~~*You must not to park here.*~~

5 We use **You must not** to say that it is necessary that somebody does NOT do something:
***You must not smoke** in here.*
***You must not make** this mistake again.*

We use **I/We must not ...** to say that we think it is necessary that we do NOT do something:
***I must not forget** her birthday again.*
***We must not be** late for the meeting.*

6 Notice that we can use **must** and **must not** (NOT ~~**will must**~~) to talk about the future:
I must call Harry tomorrow.
(NOT ~~I will must call~~ ...)

To talk about what was necessary in the past, we cannot use **must**; we use a form of **have to.**

We don't generally use **must** in a question form. We use **have to.**

Practice

A The Hotel Strict is not a very nice hotel. It has a lot of rules. Read the list of rules, and change each one into a sentence using *must* or *must not*.

Notice to guests
Leave your key at reception when you go out.
Do not call room service before 9 a.m.
Leave your room neat and tidy.
Wipe your feet before you enter.
Do not use the pool after 8 p.m.
Pay for your room when you arrive.

► You must leave .... your key at reception when you go out.
1 You .... room service before 9 a.m.
2 .... your room neat and tidy.
3 .... your feet before you enter.
4 .... the pool after 8 p.m.
5 .... for your room when you arrive.

B **Look at this table of instructions at a gym. Use the table to write sentences with *must* or *must not*.**

	Yes	No
Wear clean shoes.	✓	
Bring your own water bottle.	✓	
Talk during the yoga class.		✓
Show your card when you arrive.	✓	
Wipe the machines after using them.	✓	
Leave items in the lockers overnight.		✓

► You must wear............ clean shoes.
1 .... your own water bottle.
2 .... during the yoga class.
3 .... your card when you arrive.
4 .... the machines after using them.
5 .... items in the lockers overnight.

C **Henry wants to make some changes in his life. Look at the pictures and write sentences using the phrases in the box with *must* or *must not.***

study in the evening	run every morning	~~dress well~~	watch TV all day
~~smoke~~	visit my grandmother	sleep in the afternoon	dance all night

► I must not smoke.

► I must dress well.......

1........................

2........................

3........................

4........................

5........................

6........................

D **Rewrite the sentences in parentheses ( ) using *must* or *must not*.**

► (Have some of this fish. It's wonderful.)
You must have some of this fish.............................. . It's wonderful.
1 (Don't tell lies. It's bad.)
You .... It's bad.
2 (Passengers: Do not open the door while the train is moving.)
Passengers .... while the train is moving.
3 (Go out for dinner with us one evening next week!)
You .... one evening next week!
4 (All staff: show identity cards when you enter the building.)
All staff .... when they enter the building.
5 (It's bad for you to eat so much unhealthy food.)
You .... so much unhealthy food.
6 (Follow the instructions when using this machine.)
You .... when using this machine.

Have to

1 The Simple Present forms of **have to** are:

POSITIVE and NEGATIVE		
I/You/We/They	have / don't have	to go.
He/She/It	has / doesn't have	to go.
QUESTIONS		
Do I/you/we/they	have	to go?
Does he/she/it	have	to go?

2 We use **have to** to talk about things that are necessary because of rules that other people oblige us to follow:

My brother ***has to travel*** *a lot for his job.* (It is required by his employer.)

We ***have to pay*** *the rent every month.* (It is required by the landlord.)

To talk about things that WE think are necessary, we usually use **must**.

3 We also use **have to** for things that are necessary because of the circumstances:

I ***have to take*** *a bus to school.* (It is the only way I can travel there.)

She ***has to live*** *on a small income.* (She only receives a small amount of money to pay for what she needs.)

4 We use **don't have to** to say that something is NOT necessary.

We ***don't have to hurry****; we're early.* (= It's not necessary to hurry. We have plenty of time.)

I ***don't have to get*** *up early on Sunday.* (I can stay in bed if I want.)

5 We can use **have got to** with the same meaning as **have to** to talk about something that is necessary at one particular time (but not in general):

I ***have to/I've got to make*** *a phone call now.*

You ***don't have to/haven't got to do*** *this immediately.*

6 The past form of **have to** is **had to:**

I ***had to do*** *a lot of work yesterday.*

7 The future form of **have to** is **will have to:**

*He'***ll have to look*** *for another job.*

We ***won't have to get*** *tickets in advance.*

Will *they* ***have to get*** *passports?*

Note that we cannot use **have got to** in past or future forms:

Yesterday I ***had to work*** *hard.* (NOT ~~*I had got to work hard.*~~)

8 We can use the Simple Present of **have to** to talk about the future:

I ***have to do*** *some shopping tomorrow.*

Do you ***have to work*** *next weekend?*

Practice

A **Look at this table about different jobs and use the information to complete the sentences, using *have to* or *don't have to*.**

	Waiters	Bank tellers	Doctors	Teachers
deal with the public	✓	✓	✓	✗
be polite to people	✓	✓	✗	✗
work with money	✓	✓	✗	✗
wear uniforms	✓	✗	✓	✗

► Waiters *have to deal*.................. with the public.
1 Teachers .... to people.
2 Bank tellers .... to people.
3 Bank tellers .... with money.
4 Doctors .... with money.

5 Waiters often .... uniforms.
6 Teachers .... uniforms.

B **Complete the sentences using the correct forms of *have to* or *have got to* and the words in parentheses ( ). Be careful to use the correct tense.**

► *I have to leave* .... (I/leave) now; I've got an appointment at the dentist.
► *Did you have to study* .... (you/study) literature when you were at school?
► *You've got to come* .... (You/come) with me now.
1 .... (I/not/work) hard because the job was very easy.
2 .... (I/do) this work now, or can I do it tomorrow?
3 .... (I/run) to school because I was late.
4 .... (I/go) to an important meeting yesterday.
5 .... (you/show) your passports when you reached the border?
6 .... (I/pay) in cash next week or can I give you a cheque?
7 I want to be an airline pilot. What qualifications .... (you/have) to be a pilot?
8 .... (You/not/decide) today. You can tell me tomorrow.
9 I arrived late yesterday because .... (I/wait) a long time for a bus.
10 A: .... (you/work) every weekend?
B: No, I don't; but .... (I/work) last weekend.

C **Complete the conversations, using the correct forms of *have to* or *have got to*.**

A: (Good morning, I'd like to buy a student discount card. What/I/do?)
(►) *Good morning. I'd like to buy a student discount card. What do I have to do?*
B: (You/fill/in an application form.)
(1) ....
A: (I/give/you/a photograph?)
(2) ....
B: (No, you/not/give/me anything, except the money for the card.)
(3) ....

Dad: (What/you/do/at school today?)
(►) *What did you have to do at school today?*
Geoff: (We/do/some/French tests.)
(4) ....
Dad: (How many questions/you/answer?)
(5) ....
Geoff: (We/answer/about forty grammar questions.)
(6) ....
(I/think/about them very carefully.)
(7) ....
Dad: (you/write/an essay?)
(8) ....
Geoff: (No, but we/do/one next week.)
(9) ....

Should, shouldn't

1 We use **should** with an infinitive (**do, go,** etc.):

INFINITIVE
I ***should*** **do** *some work tonight.*

The form of **should** is the same for all persons:

I/You/He/She/It/We/They **should go.**

2 The negative form is **shouldn't:**

You ***shouldn't*** *sit in the sun all day.*
They ***shouldn't*** *spend so much money.*

3 We use **I should** or **we should** to say what is a good thing for us to do:

I ***should go*** *home. It's midnight.*
We ***should invite*** *them for dinner.*

We use **I** or **we shouldn't** to say that something is a bad thing for us to do:

I ***shouldn't*** *spend so much money.*

We use **you should/shouldn't** to give advice:

You ***should look*** *for a better job.*
You ***shouldn't drive*** *so fast.*

Should is not as strong as **must** or **have to.** Compare:

You ***should eat*** *more fruit.* (It's a good idea.)
"You ***must eat*** *more fruit," said the doctor.* (It's very important).

4 We use the question form **should I/we ...?** to ask for advice:

What ***should I say*** *to Alison?*
I need a new passport. Where ***should I*** *go?*

5 We can say **I think we should, I don't think you should,** etc. to give an opinion:

I don't think you should believe *everything he says.*

We do not usually say:
~~*I think you shouldn't*~~ ...

6 We can use **do you think I should ...?** to ask for advice:

He hasn't replied to my email. ***Do you think I should call*** *him?*
What ***do you think I should give*** *Chris for his birthday?*

Practice

A Complete the sentences using *should* or *shouldn't* and the words in parentheses ( ).

► *You shouldn't work* .... (You/work) so hard. Take a vacation.
► I enjoyed that movie. *We should go* .... (We/go) to the theatre more often.
1 .... (You/park) here. It's not allowed.
2 What .... (I/cook) for dinner tonight?
3 .... (You/wear) a coat. It's cold outside.
4 .... (You/smoke). It's bad for you.
5 .... (We/arrive) at the airport two hours before the flight.
6 .... (I/pay) now or later?
7 Do you think .... (I/apply) for this job?
8 What do you think .... (I/write) in this space on the form?
9 .... (I/eat) any more cake. I've already eaten too much.
10 This food is terrible. .... (We/complain) to the manager.
11 Which shirt do you think .... (I/buy)?

B **Daryl is cooking a meal. Give him some useful advice. Use *you should* or *you shouldn't* and the notes in the box.**

> Don't leave the beef in the oven for more than one hour.
> Cut the onions as small as possible.
> Use fresh herbs and fresh vegetables.
> Don't add too much salt and pepper.
> Wait until the water boils before you put the vegetables in it.
> Heat the oven before you put the beef in.
> Cut the beef into four equal pieces.

► You shouldn't leave........ the beef in the oven for more than one hour.
1 .... the onions as small as possible.
2 .... fresh herbs and fresh vegetables.
3 .... too much salt and pepper.
4 .... until the water boils before you put the vegetables in it.
5 .... the oven before you put the beef in.
6 .... the beef into four equal pieces.

C **Write this conversation between Brian and Keith using the words in parentheses ( ). Write *do* or *should* where required.**

Brian: (I want to buy a motorcycle. What/you/think/I/do?)
(►) I want to buy a motorcycle. What do you think I should do?............................
Keith: (You/look/at the ads in the newspapers.)
(►) You should look at the ads in the newspapers...
Brian: (Which papers/I/get?)
(1)..
Keith: (I think/you/buy/the local newspapers.)
(2)..
Brian: (What/you/think/I/do/before I buy a bike?)
(3)..
Keith: (I/not/think/you/decide/too quickly.)
(4)..
(You/check/the condition of the bike.)
(5)..
(You/ask/somebody who knows about bikes to look at the bike for you.)
(6)..
(You/not/buy/one simply because it looks nice!)
(7)..
(You/be/very careful.)
(8)..

Can/Could I? May I? Can/Could you?

1 We form questions with **can, may,** and **could** like this:

QUESTIONS		
Can / May / Could	I/he/she/it/we (etc.)	wait?

2 We use **can, may,** and **could** to ask for things:

Can etc.	+ I/we	+ have	... ?
Can	*I*	*have*	*a coffee?*

Could we **have** *two tickets, please?*
Can I **have** *some sugar?*

3 We use **can, may,** or **could** to ask for permission. **Could I** and **May I** are more formal and polite than **Can I:**

Can/May/Could	+ I/we	+ INFINITIVE	...?
May	*I*	*see*	*her?*

***Could** we **look** at your map, please?*
***Can** I **borrow** your hockey stick, please?*

We use **can** or **may** to give permission:
*You **can** leave your purse here.* (OR ... ***may** leave* ...)

If we talk about what is allowed in general, rather than by a particular person, we use **can:**
*People **can** drive when they are sixteen.*

But official notices often use **may:**
PURSES MAY BE LEFT HERE.

4 We use **Can you, Could you,** and **Would you** (but not ~~May you~~) when we ask someone to do something. **Could** and **would** are more formal and polite than **can.**

Can/Could/Would	+ you	+ INFINITIVE	...?
Could	*you*	*help*	*me?*

A: *I'm cold.* ***Can** you **close** the window?*
B: *Yes, of course.*

Practice

A Write the words in parentheses ( ) in the correct order to make questions.

► (have – a round-trip ticket to Edmonton – could – please – I – ?)
Could I have a round-trip ticket to Edmonton, please?

1 (please – I – may – a glass of orange juice – have – ?)
....

2 (we – watch that movie – can – ?)
....

3 (your cellphone – please – use – I – can – ?)
....

4 (may – borrow – your camera tomorrow – I – ?)
....

5 (please – the maple syrup – pass – you – could – ?)
....

6 (can – this letter for me – you – mail – ?)
....

B Ask for permission. Use the words in parentheses ( ) and the words in the box.

borrow your notes	~~use your dictionary~~	use your computer
see the newspaper	have the window seat	

▶ SITUATION: You want to find the meaning of a word.
(may I) May I use your dictionary?

1 SITUATION: You want to check your email.
(may I) ....

2 SITUATION: You want to read about today's news.
(can I … please) ....

3 SITUATION: You missed a class yesterday.
(may I) ....

4 SITUATION: You want to see the scenery during a train ride.
(can I … please) ....

C Ask people to do things. Use the words in parentheses ( ) and the phrases in the box.

~~buy me a magazine~~	switch seats with me	heat this up
lend me five dollars	turn up the heat	

▶ PROBLEM: You're sick. You're in bed. You're bored.
(can you … please) Can you buy me a magazine, please?

1 PROBLEM: You're at a movie and someone tall sits in front of you.
(could you) ....

2 PROBLEM: Your dinner is cold.
(could you … please) ....

3 PROBLEM: You need to buy milk, but you've forgotten your money.
(can you) ....

4 PROBLEM: You're at a friend's house and you feel cold.
(can you … please) ....

D Choose the correct word from the words in parentheses ( ) and write it in the blank.

▶ Could (May/Could) you give me one of these forms, please?

1 On the street:
Excuse me, officer, ... (could/may) you tell me how to get to the subway station?

2 At a train station:
A: Let's have our sandwiches here.
B: .... (Couldn't/Can't) you read? Look at the notice; it says:
"FOOD .... (MAY/COULD) NOT BE EATEN IN THIS WAITING ROOM."

3 A: .... (Could/May) you call Jenny about tomorrow's meeting?
B: I .... (may not/can't/couldn't) call her because she has lost her cellphone.

4 A: .... (May/Could) someone help me?
B: What .... (may/can) I do to help you?
A: We need to move the chairs and to clean this room. Can you help?
B: I'm afraid I .... (may not/can't) move the chairs because of my bad back.

Passive sentences

1 We form the Simple Present passive like this:

	am/is/are	+ PAST PARTICIPLE	
Glass	*is*	*made*	*from sand.*

POSITIVE AND NEGATIVE

This series ***is shown*** *on TV every Thursday.*
These computers ***aren't produced*** *any more.*

QUESTIONS

When ***is*** *breakfast* ***served*** *in this hotel?*

(For information on the forms of regular past participles, see Appendix 2, page 95, and for irregular past participles, see Appendix 3, page 96.)

2 We form the Simple Past passive like this:

	was/were	+	PAST PARTICIPLE	
Anna	*was*		*born*	*in Germany.*

POSITIVE AND NEGATIVE

Romeo and Juliet ***was written*** *by Shakespeare.*
The goods ***weren't delivered*** *yesterday.*

QUESTIONS

When ***was*** *your camera* ***stolen?***

3 Look at these sentences:

ACTIVE: *They sell* [OBJECT *cold drinks*] *here.*
PASSIVE: [*Cold drinks* SUBJECT] *are sold here.*

Notice that the object in the active sentence (**cold drinks**) is the same as the subject in the passive sentence. We use the passive when it is not important who does the action, or when we don't know who does it:

These cars are made in Japan. (We don't need to say … ~~by Japanese workers~~.)
This house was built in the eighteenth century. (We don't know who built it.)

4 Now look at these examples:

(i) ***Alfred Hitchcock*** *was a great filmmaker.* ***He*** *directed this film in 1956.*
(ii) *This is a wonderful* ***film. It*** *was directed by Alfred Hitchcock.*

In (ii) we use the passive because we have been talking about something (**the film**), and not the person who did it (**Hitchcock**). We use **by** to say who does, or did, the action:

This film was directed ***by*** *Hitchcock.*

Practice

A Complete these sentences using the correct form of the verbs from the box. Use the passive form of the Simple Present or Simple Past.

write	sell	~~fix~~	bite	give	find	~~make~~	watch	tell	pay

► Scotch whiskey is made............... in Scotland.
► The car was fixed............ last week.
1 Sophia .... not to make a mess in the kitchen.
2 *The Handmaid's Tale* .... in the 1980s.
3 Abdul .... by a snake while we were hiking.
4 Firefighters .... by the city.
5 This show .... by ten million people every week.
6 His painting .... for $10,000.
7 This wallet .... outside the museum.
8 I .... a speeding ticket for driving too fast.

B Now write the questions for the sentences in exercise A, using the passive form.

- ► Where is Scotch whiskey made? ....
- ► When was the car fixed? ....
1. What ....
2. When ....
3. Who ....
4. Who ....
5. How many ....
6. How much ....
7. Where ....
8. Why ....

C Change the active sentences into passive sentences. Use the words in parentheses ( ).

- ► We sell tickets for all shows at the box office. (Tickets for all shows/sell/at the box office)
  Tickets for all shows are sold at the box office. ....
1. Muni gave me this ruby bracelet. (ruby bracelet/give/to me/by Muni)
   ....
2. Jeff planted a vegetable garden. (vegetable garden/plant/by Jeff)
   ....
3. They don't collect garbage on weekends. (garbage/not/collect/weekends)
   ....
4. Someone painted this fence white. (fence/paint/white)
   ....
5. A nurse picked up the baby. (baby/pick up/by a nurse)
   ....
6. Someone wrote this letter last week. (letter/write/last week)
   ....

D Write the correct active or passive form in parentheses ( ).

Fiat (►) was started........ (started/was started) by a group of Italian businessmen in 1899. In 1903, Fiat (1)........................ (produced/was produced) 132 cars. Some of these cars (2)........................ (exported/were exported) by the company to the United States and Britain. In 1920, Fiat (3)........................ (started/was started) making cars at a new factory at Lingotto, near Turin. There was a track on the roof where the cars (4)........................ (tested/were tested) by technicians. In 1936, Fiat launched the Fiat 500. This car (5)........................ (called/was called) the Topolino – the Italian name for Mickey Mouse. The company grew, and in 1963 Fiat (6)........................ (exported/was exported) more than 300,000 vehicles. Today, Fiat is based in Turin, and its cars (7)........................ (sold/are sold) all over the world.

Verb + **-ing; like** and **would like**

1 Look at this example:

	-ing FORM	
I like	***listening***	*to music.*

(For details on **-ing** forms, see Appendix 2, page 95.)

We can use certain verbs (e.g. **like**) with an **-ing** form:

like	**enjoy**	**love**	**keep**	+ **-ing** FORM
finish	**stop**	**mind**	**hate**	

*She doesn't **like cooking**.*
*Do you **enjoy driving**?*
*They **love living** in Quebec.*
*He **keeps saying** the same things.*
(= He says the same things many times.)
*Have you **finished eating**?*
*Suddenly she **stopped talking**.*
*I don't **mind waiting**.*

2 Compare this pair of sentences:

> *I **like working** here.* (= I enjoy my job here.)
> *I'**d like*** (= I **would like**) *to get a better job.*
> (= I want to get a better job.)

We use **like + -ing** (e.g. **like listening, like working**) to talk about things that we enjoy doing. We use **would like to** to say that we want to do something. Here are some more examples:

*She **likes painting** pictures.* (= She enjoys painting pictures.)
*She **would like to be** an artist.*
(= She wants to be an artist.)
*I **like going** to the theatre.*
(= I enjoy going to the theatre.)
*I'**d like to go** to the theatre tonight.*
(= I want to go to the theatre tonight.)
*Do you **like playing** cards?*
(= Do you enjoy playing cards?)
***Would** you **like to play** cards now?*
(= Do you want to play now?)

In offers and requests it is more polite to say **would like** than **want**:

***Would** you **like to come** for dinner?* (offer)
*I'**d like to leave** work early, please.* (request)

3 We use **go + -ing** for sports and hobbies that we go out to do, and with shopping:

*We often **go skiing** in the winter.*
*Let's **go swimming** this afternoon.*
*She **goes dancing** on weekends.*
*I'm **going shopping** this afternoon.*

4 We can use the **-ing** form of a verb as the subject of a sentence to talk about activities:

***Swimming** is a healthy activity.*

In sentences like this, we can use a noun, adverb, or prepositional phrase after the **-ing** form:

***Riding** snowmobiles can be dangerous.*
***Exercising** regularly is good for you.*
***Dancing** to this kind of music can be difficult.*

Practice

A **Complete the sentences using a Simple Present form of the first verb in parentheses ( ) and the *-ing* form of the second verb.**

► She likes playing.................. (like/play) tennis, but she .doesn't like watching...... (not/like/watch) it.

1 The buses .... (stop/run) at midnight.
2 I .... (not/mind/listen) to his problems.
3 He's not very good at playing chess, so he .... (keep/lose).
4 She .... (enjoy/go) to other countries and she .... (like/meet) new people.
5 I .... (keep/make) the same stupid mistakes!
6 They usually .... (finish/eat) at about eight-thirty at night.
7 She .... (not/enjoy/drive), but she .... (love/cycle).

B **Complete the sentences using *like/not like + -ing* or *would like + to* with the words in parentheses ( ).**

► She doesn't like working........ (work) here. She hates this job and is going to look for a better one.
► Would you like to watch... (you/watch) a different show, or do you want to watch this one?
1 I .... (live) here. I have lived here for many years and I think it's a nice town.
2 Sarah .... (be) a journalist when she finishes university. She wants to work for a newspaper or a magazine.
3 I .... (get up) so early every morning, but I have to do it.
4 I .... (go out) for dinner in an Italian restaurant tonight.
5 Clare .... (find) a job in Alberta. She wants to work in Calgary or Edmonton.
6 I .... (watch) television all the time; I think it's a waste of time.
7 Sasha .... (lie) on the beach when she's on vacation. She doesn't like swimming or going on day trips.

C **Look at the pictures. They show what John did last week on vacation. Complete the sentences using the correct form of *go* and a verb from the box.**

dance ~~shop~~ sail swim ski cycle

►

Monday

1

Tuesday

2

Wednesday

3

Thursday

4

Friday

5

Saturday

► On Monday he went shopping.............
1 On Tuesday ....
2 On Wednesday ....
3 On Thursday ....
4 On Friday ....
5 On Saturday ....

D **Write the *-ing* form of one of these verbs in each sentence:**

eat	play	~~walk~~	drive

► Walking...... in the provincial park is very nice at this time of year.
1 .... the guitar is his favourite hobby.
2 .... on busy highways can be very tiring.
3 .... unhealthy things all the time is bad for you.

Infinitive with/without **to**

1 Look at this example:

I want **to buy** *some stamps.* (to + INFINITIVE)

We use **to do, to buy, to start,** etc. (**to** + infinitive) after some verbs, e.g.:

want	decide	
agree	promise	
forget	offer	+ to + INFINITIVE
hope	plan	
arrange	try	

She ***agreed to lend*** *him some money.*
He ***forgot to buy*** *the tickets.*
I'm ***hoping to get*** *a new bike soon.*
I've ***arranged to play*** *tennis tonight.*
They've ***decided to start*** *a new company.*
You ***promised to help*** *me.*
She ***offered to do*** *the dishes.*
We're ***planning to go*** *away this weekend.*
He's ***trying to learn*** *French.*

2 We can also say **want + someone + to:**
His parents ***want him to go*** *to university.*
Do you ***want me to help*** *you?*

3 Now look at this example:

He ***can*** ***speak*** *Spanish.* (INFINITIVE)

Can is a modal verb. We use **do, speak, see,** etc. (infinitives) after a modal verb. Some of the most common modal verbs are:

will ('ll) should may might can could must	+ INFINITIVE

*I'**ll see** you soon.*
She ***won't agree.***
Where ***should I sit?***
We ***can go*** *by train.*
It ***may not cost*** *much.*
Can I park *here?*
I ***couldn't hear*** *her.*
We ***must pay*** *now.*

4 We can use **make + someone + infinitive,** to mean "cause" or "force":
The movie ***made me cry.***
(= It caused me to cry.)
They ***made us leave.***
(= They forced us to leave.)

5 We can use **let + someone + infinitive,** to mean "allow":
She ***let me stay.*** (= She allowed me to stay.)

Practice

A Write the verbs in parentheses ( ) in these sentences. Use an infinitive (*call*) or *to + infinitive* (*to call*).

► You can't smoke........ (smoke) here. Smoking is not allowed in restaurants.
1 I'm sorry I forgot .... (call) you yesterday. I was very busy.
2 Don't worry. The test may not .... (be) very difficult.
3 Her mother makes her .... (clean) her room.
4 It's not a very good movie. You won't .... (enjoy) it.
5 She didn't want .... (wait) any longer, so she left.
6 When are you planning .... (eat) tonight?
7 She couldn't .... (reply) because she didn't know what to say.
8 This kind of music makes me .... (feel) good.
9 My friend let me .... (drive) her car.
10 I'm afraid I've forgotten .... (bring) the map.
11 They might not .... (receive) the letter until next week.

B **Complete each sentence so that it has the same meaning as the sentence in parentheses ( ).**

► (I don't think it's a good idea to argue with him.)
I don't think you should *argue with him.* ....
1 (I won't be able to go to the meeting on Friday.)
I can't ....
2 (I'm meeting some friends tonight.)
I've arranged ....
3 (Listen to what I'm telling you.)
I want you ....
4 (It's important that you lock the door when you go out.)
Don't forget ....
5 (Perhaps we'll go out for dinner tonight.)
We may ....
6 (Allow me to pay for the meal.)
Let ....
7 (I'd like to take a course in art history.)
I want ....
8 (He said, "I'll pay the bill.")
He offered ....
9 (Should I sit in this chair?)
Do you want me ....
10 (His stories were very funny, and I laughed a lot.)
His funny stories made ....
11 (Perhaps he'll call you tomorrow.)
He might ....
12 (It's possible that Mathieu won't be angry with you.)
Mathieu might not ....
13 (Jane allowed me to drive her new car.)
Jane let ....

C **Complete the conversation, using the verbs in parentheses ( ) with or without *to*.**

Charlie: I want (►) *to do*.................. (do) something interesting this weekend. Can we (1)........................ (do) something together?
Carol: Well, I've arranged (2)........................ (go) on a trip to Quebec City with some friends. Do you want (3)........................ (come) with us?
Charlie: Yes, that sounds good. When are you planning (4)........................ (leave)?
Carol: Well, we've decided (5)........................ (start) early in the morning tomorrow, and I've promised (6)........................ (take) the others in my car. We're hoping (7)........................ (reach) Quebec City by lunchtime. So, you must (8)........................ (meet) me here at six a.m.
Charlie: OK, good. I won't (9)........................ (be) late.

Reported speech

1 When we report something that somebody said, we usually change the tense of the verb like this:

ACTUAL WORDS	REPORTED SPEECH
Simple Present → "I *live* in a small apartment," she said.	Simple Past — *She said she* ***lived*** *in a small apartment.*
Present Progressive → *"I'm* ***leaving*** *on Tuesday," I said.*	Past Progressive — *I said that I* ***was leaving*** *on Tuesday.*
Simple Past / Present Perfect } → *"I* ***learned*** *a lot," he said.* *"Mr. Jackson* ***has left****," she said.*	Past Perfect — *He said he* ***had learned*** *a lot.* ***She said that*** *Mr. Jackson* ***had left****.*
will → *"I'll* ***help*** *you," she said.*	would — *She said she* ***would help*** *me.*
am/is/are going to → *"We're* ***going to be*** *late," I said.*	was/were going to — *I said that we* ***were going to be*** *late.*
can → *"I* ***can't find*** *my money," he said.*	could — *He said he* ***couldn't find*** *his money.*

2 Note that it is not necessary to use **that** in reported speech:

*She said (**that**) she knew the answer.*

3 Compare **say** and **tell** in these sentences:

*She **said** (that) she lived in a small apartment.*
*She **told me** (that) she lived in a small apartment.*

We **say something.** We do not **say someone something.**

She said she was going to be late.
(NOT ~~*She said me she was*~~ ...)
I said that I disagreed with him.
(NOT ~~*I said him that I*~~ ...)

We **tell someone something.** We do not **tell something.**

*He told **me** he was happy.*
(NOT ~~*He told he was happy.*~~)
*He told **me** that he would pay me immediately.*
(NOT ~~*He told that he would pay me immediately.*~~)
*She told **Fred** she was going to meet someone.*
(NOT ~~*She told that she was going to meet someone.*~~)

Practice

A Look at these pictures of people coming through passport control at an airport. Change the things they said into reported speech.

► He said *that he was visiting friends.* ....
1 She said ....
2 He said ....
3 They said ....
4 She said ....

B **Read this conversation and then report what Rosie and Mary Ellen said.**

Rosie: How long have you been in France?
Mary Ellen: Six weeks.
Rosie: Has the weather been nice?
Mary Ellen: Yes, it rained only twice.
Rosie: What have you been doing for fun?
Mary Ellen: I bought a bike and I'm riding around Paris every day.
Rosie: Have you been to the Louvre?
Mary Ellen: Not yet. I'm going on Thursday.
Rosie: I'd like to go, too.
Mary Ellen: OK, you can go with me!
Rosie: What time should we go to the museum?
Mary Ellen: I'll meet you at your hotel at nine.
Rosie: How far is the museum from my hotel?
Mary Ellen: It's only about four blocks away.
Rosie: Should I take anything with me?
Mary Ellen: Just wear some comfortable shoes. We'll be walking a lot.
Rosie: Great. I'll see you then!

► Mary Ellen said (that) she had been .... in France for six weeks.
1 Mary Ellen said .... only twice.
2 Mary Ellen said .... a bike and .... around Paris every day.
3 Mary Ellen said .... to the Louvre.
4 She said .... on Thursday.
5 She said .... to the Louvre with her.
6 She said .... Rosie at the hotel at nine.
7 She said .... walking a lot.

C **Complete the sentences with *said* or *told*.**

► She said .... she wasn't feeling very well.
1 Jason .... us that he was getting married.
2 Hayley .... that she was excited about the party.
3 Marina .... that she had finished reading the book.
4 Nadine .... Susan how to fix the flat tire.
5 Katie .... everyone about the surprise party.
6 Cindy .... that it had started to snow.
7 Julie .... them that she was going to Mexico.
8 Matt .... that he wanted to learn to ski.
9 Carrie .... that the coffee wasn't hot enough.
10 Jeff .... his sister that she should go back to school.

Articles: **a/an**, **the**, or no article

1 We use **a/an** with singular nouns:
*He was reading **a** book.*
*I saw **an** interesting movie yesterday.*

2 Look at this example:
*When I arrived, John was reading **a book**.*

We use **a/an** when it isn't necessary to make clear which specific thing we are talking about. There are lots of books; John was reading one of them.

We use **a/an** to talk about people's jobs:
*Jim is **an engineer**.* (= There are lots of engineers; Jim is one.)

We use **a/an** to describe things or people:
*They have **a beautiful house**.* (= There are lots of beautiful houses; they have one.)
*John is **an old friend** of mine.*

3 We use **the** with singular or plural nouns:
***the** book* ***the** books*

We can use **the** with uncountable nouns (e.g. **music, water, food, snow**):
***The water** is in the fridge.*

Note:
- uncountable nouns do not have a plural (NOT ~~two musics~~, ~~three waters~~).
- we do not use **a/an** with uncountable nouns (NOT ~~a music~~, ~~a water~~).

4 We use **the** when it is clear which person or thing we are talking about:
*Karen was reading **a** book. She closed **the book**.* (= She closed the book that she was reading.)
*Anna likes music, but she doesn't like **the music** that John plays.*
*Mike's gone to **the mall**.* (= the local mall)
*She's in **the kitchen**.* (= the kitchen in this house)
*I must go to **the bank**.* (= my bank, where I keep my money)
the bus station/the airport (in a city)
the Fraser River (There is only one.)
***the government** in my country*

5 We do not use **the** before plural nouns (e.g. **vegetables**) or uncountable nouns (e.g. **education, music**) when we are talking about something in general:
*Do you like **vegetables**?* (= any vegetables)
*I think **education** is very important.*

6 We do not use **a** or **the** before names of languages, meal names, the names of cities, most countries and most streets, and the names of airports, stations, single mountains, or lakes:
*She speaks **Spanish**.*
*She lives in **Amsterdam**, in **Holland**.* (But we say **the** United States, **the** European Union.)
*What time will **lunch** be?*
*from **Mount Lucania** to **Kluane Lake***

Practice

A Write *a*, *an*, or *the* in the blanks if they are required. Leave the blank empty if nothing is required.

► I want to put some money into my bank account, so I'm going to the........... bank this afternoon. It's on King Street.
1 I saw Lee today. He just bought .... house in .... Vancouver.
2 Have you heard .... news? There's a fire downtown!
3 Do you like .... movies? There's .... new comedy playing at .... theatre on .... Charles Street.
4 Francine lives in .... apartment with her friends.
5 I can speak .... French and .... English.
6 I can't believe what happened during .... game last night! .... goalie scored a goal.

B **Complete the sentences by writing *a*, *an*, or *the* if required. Leave the blank empty if nothing is required. (Note that the following words in this exercise are uncountable nouns: *butter*, *water*, *energy*.)**

► She read *the*.... emails she had received that morning.
1 Monica set .... table for .... breakfast.
2 Please pass .... butter, please.
3 I'm taking .... vacation next month. I'm going to .... Jamaica.
4 Hydroelectricity uses .... water to create .... energy.
5 Jesse doesn't like .... vegetables. He rarely eats them.
6 Would you like .... piece of pie?
7 Have you read .... book that George wrote?
8 I think .... bar is closed. We should go to the other one down .... street.
9 I hear .... phone ringing. Is it yours?
10 He hasn't spoken .... Spanish since he left .... Peru two years ago.

C **Complete this conversation by writing *a*, *an*, or *the* if required. Leave the blank empty if nothing is required.**

Mike: Is Maria (►) *a*...... student at your college?
Rosie: No, she's (1)........ old friend of mine. We were in school together.
Mike: What does she do now?
Rosie: She's (2)........ computer programmer. She's not Canadian, you know. She comes from (3)........ Brazil, but she's living in (4)........ US at the moment.
Mike: Has she got (5)........ job there?
Rosie: Yes, she's working for (6)........ big company there.
Mike: Do you send (7)........ emails to each other?
Rosie: Yes, and I had (8)........ long email from her yesterday.
Mike: What did she say in (9)........ email?
Rosie: She said that she was living in (10)........ nice apartment in (11)........ middle of (12)........ Chicago.

D **Complete the story by writing *a*, *an*, or *the* in the blanks.**

Yesterday I was walking through (►) *the*.... park, when I saw (1)........ large dog running toward me. I tried to get out of (2)........ way, but I was too late. (3)........ dog knocked me into (4)........ mud puddle! At first, I was angry, but then I saw (5)........ dog's owner. She was (6)........ older woman with (7)........ cane, who was struggling to keep up with her energetic dog. She apologized for what (8)........ dog had done, I told her that it was okay, and then we went for (9)........ nice walk together.

Myself, **yourself**, etc.; **each other**

1 Look at this table:

SUBJECT PRONOUNS	OBJECT PRONOUNS	REFLEXIVE PRONOUNS
I	me	myself
you (*singular*)	you	yourself
he	him	himself
she	her	herself
it	it	itself
we	us	ourselves
you (*plural*)	you	yourselves
they	them	themselves

2 Compare:

(i)

Jenny made Jo a cup of coffee.
(= Jenny made the coffee for Jo.)

(ii)

Jenny made ***herself*** *a cup of coffee.*
(= Jenny made the coffee for herself.)

We use **myself, yourself, herself**, etc. to refer to the subject:

SUBJECT
Be careful. ***You*** *might hurt* ***yourself.***

I bought ***myself*** *a new shirt.*
He taught ***himself*** *to skate.*
They enjoyed ***themselves*** *at the concert.*

3 We also use **myself, yourself**, etc. to emphasize that the subject did the action, not another person:
He built the whole house ***himself.***
(= He built it alone; nobody helped him.)

4 We use **each other** like this:
Pierre and Sue were talking to each other.
(= Pierre was talking to Sue, and Sue was talking to Pierre.)
We like ***each other*** *very much.*
(= I like her and she likes me.)

Compare **themselves** and **each other:**
Alan and Ruth took these photographs ***themselves.*** (= They took them, not another person.)
Alan and Ruth took photographs of ***each other.*** (= Alan took a photograph of Ruth, and Ruth took a photograph of Alan.)

Practice

A Fill in the blanks with a reflexive pronoun (*myself*, *yourself*, etc.).

► I cooked myself........ a meal and then I watched television.
1 I'm sure he'll enjoy .... on his trip.
2 I cut .... while I was preparing the vegetables.
3 We amused .... by playing cards while we were waiting for the plane.
4 She put the plates on the table and told the guests to help .... to the food.
5 Gino hurt .... when he was playing football.
6 Adeel made .... a snack when he got home.

B Complete the sentences with the correct verb tenses and a reflexive pronoun (*myself*, *yourself*, etc.) in the correct place.

► (Be careful with that knife or you/cut/.)
Be careful with that knife or you'll cut yourself.. .
1 (It was a very nice trip and we/enjoy/very much.)
It was a very nice trip and we ....

2 (I/burn/while I was taking the dish out of the oven.)
I .... while I was taking the dish out of the oven.

3 (He didn't take lessons. He/teach/.)
He didn't take lessons. ....

4 (I think I/buy/a new coat tomorrow.)
.... a new coat tomorrow.

5 (She/make/a sandwich and ate it in the kitchen.)
.... and ate it in the kitchen.

C Fill in the blanks with *myself*, *yourself*, etc.

► Did you paint the room yourself...... ? ~ Yes, it took me three days to do it.
1 If you won't help me, I'll have to do it all ....
2 She makes all her clothes ....
3 The students organized the concert ....
4 We painted the whole house ....
5 He wrote the letter .... and then he mailed it.

D Complete the sentences with the correct verb tenses and *myself*, *yourself*, etc. Write the reflexive pronoun at the end of the sentence.

► (She is a very successful singer. She/write/all her songs/.)
She is a very successful singer. She writes all her songs herself.........................

1 Could you mail this letter for me? ~ (No, I'm sorry, I won't have time. You/have/to mail it/.)
No, I'm sorry, I won't have time. ....

2 (Nobody helped us, so we/carry/all our luggage/.)
Nobody helped us, so ....

3 (This is an excellent photograph./you/take it/?)
This is an excellent photograph. ....

4 (She was wearing a toque that she/make/.)
She was wearing a toque that ....

5 (I hope you like the present. I/choose/it/.)
I hope you like the present. ....

6 (Do you like this meal? I/invent/the recipe/.)
Do you like this meal? ....

E Fill in the blanks with *each other*, *ourselves*, *yourselves*, or *themselves*.

► They spent the whole evening arguing with each other.......... .
► Their house is very beautiful; they designed it themselves.......... .
1 Billie-Jean met Craig in April, but they didn't see .... again until July.
2 They're not friends; in fact, they don't like .... at all.
3 Don't ask me to help you. You must do it ....
4 We didn't buy it .... A friend bought it for us.
5 I could hear two people shouting at ....
6 We're working in the same office now, so Ron and I see .... every day.

Direct and indirect objects

1 Look at this example:

(i) *She gave **her brother** the newspaper.*
(ii) *She gave the newspaper **to her brother.***

In both sentences **a newspaper** is the thing which is given, and **her brother** is the person who receives it.

2 Here are other sentences like (i):

	+ PERSON (indirect object)	+ THING (direct object)
*She **gave***	*her brother*	*a shirt.*
*He **sent***	*me*	*a letter.*
*I **showed***	*him*	*my passport.*
*Jane **lent***	*Frank*	*some money.*
*I'll **offer***	*her*	*a job.*
*I'll **cook***	*them*	*a meal.*
*I **handed***	*her*	*a plate.*
*I'll **get***	*you*	*a magazine.*
*I'll **buy***	*you*	*a cup of coffee.*

3 Here are some other sentences like (ii):
*She gave the newspaper **to her brother.***

	+ THING (direct object)	+ PERSON (to + object)
*She **gave***	*a shirt*	***to** her brother.*
*I **sent***	*postcards*	***to** my friends.*
*I **showed***	*my card*	***to** the man.*
*She **lent***	*some money*	***to** her friend.*
*He **offered***	*the doughnuts*	***to** the others.*

Note that we use **to** + object after these verbs which express the idea of giving or showing something to somebody:
give, send, show, lend, offer

But we use **for** + object after verbs which express the idea of doing something for another person:
cook, buy, get

	+ THING (direct object)	+ PERSON (for + object)
*We **cooked***	*a meal*	***for** everybody.*
*He **got***	*the newspaper*	***for** his father.*
*I'll **get***	*your book*	***for** you.*
*She **bought***	*some toys*	***for** them.*

Practice

A Put these words in the correct order to make sentences. Do not add any words.

► (He – lent – his car – Mark – .)
He lent Mark his car.

1 (a mint – Jim – She offered – .)
....

2 (Juliette – his vacation photos – He showed – .)
....

3 (them – an invitation – Have you sent – ?)
....

4 (a birthday present – Did you buy – her – ?)
....

5 (I – some of my books – a friend – gave – .)
....

6 (When you go to the post office, – some stamps – me – could you get – ?)
....

B Now write the sentences from Exercise A again, but using *to* or *for*.

► He lent his car to Mark.
1 She offered ....
2 He showed ....
3 Have you sent ....
4 Did you buy ....
5 I gave ....
6 When you go to the post office, could you get ....

C Write sentences, putting the words in parentheses ( ) in the correct place.

► She wrote a letter. (me) She wrote me a letter.
1 They sent an invitation. (us) ....
2 Sheila gave a present. (to Mike) ....
3 I made a sandwich. (her) ....
4 Donald bought a newspaper. (for Sally) ....
5 My uncle sold his camera. (me) ....
6 She left a message. (for you) ....
7 Isabel sent some flowers. (them) ....
8 Did you take the money? (to the bank) ....

D Rob and Jen went to a restaurant last night for dinner. Write sentences about what happened while they were there. Use the words in parentheses ( ).

► (The waiter/give/the menu)
(her) The waiter gave her the menu.
(to Jen) The waiter gave the menu to Jen.

1 (The waiter/got/some wine)
(them) ....
(for them) ....

2 (The waiter/show/the bottle)
(him) ....
(to Rob) ....

3 (The chef/cook/a special meal)
(them) ....
(for them) ....

4 (The waiter/give/the bill)
(Rob) ....
(to Rob) ....

5 (Jen/lend/some money, because he didn't have enough to pay the bill)
(Rob) ....
(to Rob) ....

Something, anybody, nothing, etc.

1 **something/anything** = a thing
somebody/anybody = a person
someone/anyone = a person
somewhere/anywhere = a place

2 We usually use **something, somebody, someone** and **somewhere** in positive sentences:

Something is burning. (= I can smell burning. I don't know what is burning.)
*I'm going to have **something** to eat.* (= I'm going to eat; I don't know what I'm going to eat.)
***Somebody** told me that it was a good movie.* (= A person told me it was a good movie. I can't remember who told me.)
*She lives **somewhere** up north.*

3 We usually use **anything, anybody, anyone** and **anywhere** in negative sentences, and in questions:

*I didn't know **anyone** at the party.* (= There were no people at the party who I knew.)
*I couldn't find my purse **anywhere**.* (= I couldn't find my purse in any place.)
*Did you understand **anything** she said?*

4 **nothing** = not anything
nobody/no one = not anybody/not anyone
nowhere = not anywhere

We use **nothing, nobody, no one**, and **nowhere** before or after positive verbs:

***Nothing** makes Joe unhappy.* (= There isn't anything that makes Joe unhappy.)
*There's **nothing** I want to watch on TV.*
***Nobody** was there when I arrived.*
*There is **nowhere** that I would prefer to live than Haida Gwaii.* (= There isn't anywhere …)

5 **everything** = all things
everybody/everyone = all people
everywhere = all places

We use **everything, everybody, everyone**, and **everywhere** before or after positive verbs:

***Everyone** likes music.*
*I've done **everything** I can.*

6 Note that we use a singular verb after all these words:

*Nothing **is** wrong.*
*Everyone **was** friendly.*

7 We can use **else** after **something, anybody, nowhere, everyone**, etc.:

*Let's talk about **something else**.*
(= Let's talk about a different subject.)
*I didn't tell **anybody else**.*
(= I didn't tell another person.)
*There is **nowhere else** I can look for it.*

8 We can also use an adjective (e.g. **wrong, nice**) after **something, anything**, etc.:

*Have I said **something wrong**?*

Practice

A Write the correct word from the box in each blank.

~~anything~~	nobody	everything	somebody (x2)	somewhere
nothing	everywhere	something	anyone	everyone

► She didn't say anything..... about her job when I spoke to her
1 .... called you today, but he didn't tell me his name.
2 I'm sure you'll find it .... in the house if you keep looking.
3 I had to go to the game on my own because I couldn't find .... to go with me.
4 She said that .... was fine and she was very happy.
5 Can I speak to you for a moment? I want to discuss .... with you.
6 Unfortunately, I couldn't help. There was .... I could do about the problem.

7 I looked .... but I couldn't find it.
8 She married .... she met when she was in university.
9 .... was out of the office so there was .... to answer the phone.

B Choose the correct verb form in parentheses ( ).

► I'm afraid I *don't know*.......... (know/don't know) anything about this subject.
► I rang the doorbell but nobody *was*.................. (was/wasn't) in.
1 I asked a lot of people, but nobody .... (knew/didn't know) the answer.
2 I .... (have seen/haven't seen) anything so amazing before in my life!
3 I .... (ate/didn't eat) anything for lunch yesterday.
4 Nothing interesting .... (has happened/hasn't happened) since the last time I spoke to you.
5 He loves baseball. Nothing else .... (is/isn't) important to him.
6 She .... (said/didn't say) anything about her plans for the future.

C Change each of these sentences into a new sentence with the same meaning. Use the word in parentheses ( ) with the underlined adjective or with *else*.

► A strange thing happened yesterday. (something)
Something strange....... happened yesterday.
► Let's listen to some different music. (something)
Let's listen to *something else*............. .
1 Is there an interesting show on TV tonight? (anything)
Is there .... on TV tonight?
2 You won't find better food in any other place. (anywhere)
You won't find better food ....
3 Is there a cheap place we can go for lunch? (anywhere)
Is there .... we can go for lunch?
4 Let's sit in a different place. (somewhere)
Let's sit ....
5 I'd like a hot drink. (something)
I'd like .... to drink.

D Write the correct forms of words beginning with *some-*, *any-*, *no-* or *every-* in the conversation.

Dennis: Have you read (►) *anything*..... interesting lately?
Sarah: Yes, (1)................ lent me a novel last week and I really enjoyed it.
Dennis: What was it about?
Sarah: It was about (2)................ who goes to visit Australia. She likes to go (3)................ alone. While she's travelling around on her own, (4)................ terrible happens to her. She loses (5)................ – including her passport and all her money. She doesn't know (6)................ who can help her, and she's got (7)................ to stay.
Dennis: What happens then?
Sarah: I'm not going to tell you (8)................ else! You should read the book yourself.
Dennis: It sounds like a very depressing book! I'd prefer to read (9)................ funny.
Sarah: No, read it. It's a great book. And (10)................ wonderful happens at the end.

Every/each; one/another/other/others

1 We use **every** and **each** to talk about all people or things in a group or series. In many contexts, both **every** and **each** are correct:

*The letter has been sent to **every/each** staff member.*
*We checked **every/each** item before we sent it.*

We use **every/each** + singular noun + singular verb:

***Every/Each** student has to fill in this form.*

We can use **each** (but not **every**) + **of** + **the/possessive** + **plural noun:**

*I put **each of the documents** into the correct place.*

We can use **each** (but not **every**) on its own as a subject or between a subject and a main verb:

*Tickets are now available and **each** costs the same.*
*Tickets (will) **each** cost the same.*

2 Sometimes we can only use **every**; at other times we can only use **each**. We use **every** to talk about a group or series of people or things in general, with the meaning "all of them":

***Every** ticket had been sold.*

We use **each** to talk about all individual things or people in a group or series:

***Each** ticket costs $20.*

3 We use **one** + **of** + **the/possessive** + **plural noun** to talk about one person or thing when there are several or many:

***One of the students** in my class was out sick today.*
*He is staying with **one of his relatives**.*

We can use **one** + **singular noun:**

***One flight** leaves at five p.m. and the other leaves at nine.*

We can use **one** + **singular verb:**

*There are two flights. **One leaves** at five p.m. and the other leaves at nine.*

4 We use **another** + **singular noun** with the meanings "one more" or "a different one":

*Would you like **another drink**?*
*Let's go to **another restaurant** for a change.*

Notice that we do not use **another** with **one** and a singular noun (NOT ~~*another one drink*~~).

Notice also that we do not use **another** with a plural noun (NOT ~~*I met another people*~~).

5 We use **the/possessive/quantifier** + **other** + **plural noun** with the meanings "different ones" or "ones that have not been mentioned":

***The other hotels** were more expensive.*
*Ray agreed with me but **my other friends** said I was wrong.*
*For **all other inquiries**, call this number.*

We use **the/possessive** + **other** + **singular noun** with the meaning "the one that has not already been mentioned":

*One of his sisters lives in France and **his/the other sister** lives in Australia.*

We use **the other** (**one**) to talk about a person or thing that has not already been mentioned:

*He's got two homes – one is in Toronto and **the other (one)** is in Florida.*

6 We use **others** with the meaning "other people or things":

*Some people like hockey and **others** aren't interested in it at all.*

We use **the others** with the meaning "the other people or things (in a set or group)":

*We arrived first and **the others** came later.*

Practice

A Decide whether the underlined parts of these sentences are correct or not. Put a check (✓) next to the sentences that are correct and rewrite the underlined parts of the sentences that are incorrect.

► I've told every of my friends about this. each of my friends..............................

► Each room has its own private bathroom. ✓..

1 Every house on the street is exactly the same. ....

2 Each assignment on the course have to be completed on time. ....

3 Each applicant for the job was interviewed separately. ....

4 We couldn't park because every parking lot were full. ....

5 We each paid $5 towards the cost of the food. ....

6 There are three tests and every lasts for one hour. ....

B Complete these questions, using *another*, *other*, or *others*.

► Could I ask you another...... question?

1 What time is the .... flight that day?

2 What will the .... say when I tell them about this?

3 Do you know of any .... beaches that are as good as this one?

4 Will you have .... chance to take the test?

5 Could we change our meeting to .... date?

C Complete this article about an actor, using *one*, *another*, *other*, or *others*.

William Shatner has had a remarkably successful career. (►) One.......... reason for his success is that he has such a unique acting style that he has always stood apart from (1)............... actors. (2)............... reason is, of course, his personality. In a career spanning more than 60 years, he has won several Emmys and (3)............... awards for his movie and television roles. His best-known role was Captain James T. Kirk in the series *Star Trek*, although he starred in (4)............... very popular series, *Boston Legal*, several decades later. (5)............... roles included Captain Kirk in the *Star Trek* movies, and a detective in the series *T.J. Hooker*. Although many people make fun of Shatner's acting style, the (6)............... who makes fun of it the most is Shatner himself.

D Complete these dialogues, using *one*, *another*, *other*, *the other*, *others*, or *the others*.

► A: All their flights are fully booked.
B: Well, we'll have to call another............. airline. Lots of airlines fly there.

1 A: Do you like this writer?
B: I'm not sure. I really enjoyed one of her books but I haven't enjoyed any of .... books she's written.

2 A: Have you been to any .... cities in Canada besides Vancouver?
B: Yes, on my .... visit to this country last year, I went to Calgary.

3 A: Are you on your own?
B: Yes, but .... are on their way. They'll be here soon.

4 A: Is the company you work for big?
B: It has two main offices. .... office is in Toronto and .... is in Montreal.

5 A: Can we make a decision now?
B: No, I think we should have .... discussion about the subject later.

All, most, some, none

1 We use

all/most/some + NOUN (e.g. **most cities**)

to talk about things or people in general:

*She thinks that **all sports** are boring.*
(= She thinks that every sport is boring.)
***Most cities** have a lot of stores.*
(= Almost every city has a lot of stores.)
*In **some countries** life is very hard.*
(= In a number of countries in the world, but not all or most ...)

We do not say **all/most/some + of + noun**:
Most people write tests during their lives.
(NOT ~~*Most of people*~~ ...)

2 We can also use **all** with **morning/afternoon/evening/night/day/week/year** (e.g. **all afternoon**) to mean "the whole," "from the beginning to the end of":

*They've been working hard **all day**.*
*I waited for the phone call **all morning**.*

3 We use

all/most } + **of** + **the/my/her** + NOUN
some/none }
(e.g. **all of my books**)

to talk about particular things or people:

*He spent **all of his money**.*
***Most of my friends** are interested in football.*
*I knew **some of the people** at the party.*
***None of the stores** were open.*

Notice that we use a positive verb with **none**. We can leave out **of** after **all** (but not after **most, some, none**):
*He spent **all his money**.*

4 We can use

all/most/some/none + of + it/them

when we have already mentioned the noun that **it** or **them** refers to:

*It was delicious food, but I couldn't eat **all of it**.* (**it** = the food)
*I called a number of hotels, but **most of them** were full.* (**them** = the hotels)
*That cake looks good. Can I have **some of it**?* (**it** = the cake)

Practice

A **Read these exam results for four students and complete the sentences, using *all of, some of, most of,* or *none of*. Sometimes you will need *the* (e.g. *some of the*).**

STUDENT	EXAM 1	EXAM 2	EXAM 3	EXAM 4	EXAM 5	EXAM 6
Alice	PASS	PASS	FAIL	PASS	PASS	PASS
Bill	PASS	PASS	PASS	PASS	PASS	PASS
Carol	FAIL	PASS	PASS	PASS	FAIL	FAIL
David	FAIL	FAIL	FAIL	FAIL	FAIL	FAIL

► Alice passed *most of the* .... exams.
1 Bill passed .... exams.
2 Bill failed .... them.
3 Carol passed .... exams.
4 Carol passed .... them.
5 Carol failed .... them.
6 David passed .... them.
7 David passed .... exams.
8 David failed .... exams.

B Complete the sentences by writing the correct words from the box.

all	all the	none of the	some	some of the

► All .... Canadian children have to go to school.

► The classroom is empty because some of the .... children are outside.

1 We can't buy anything today because .... the stores are closed for Labour Day.

2 We like that restaurant. .... food is expensive, but everything is very good.

3 .... people say he's the best tennis player in the world, but I don't agree.

4 That's a terrible team. .... players are any good.

5 Azim's very lazy. He reads the newspaper .... morning.

6 .... phones here are working. Can I borrow your cellphone?

7 It's a wonderful tour. You have .... day to see the sights.

8 IMPORTANT NOTICE: .... passengers must have a valid ticket.

9 If .... students can answer the teacher's questions, she explains the point again.

10 We can't sit down. .... chairs are wet.

11 .... cars use regular gas and others use diesel.

12 This light works .... time, but not always.

C Write full sentences using *all*, *most*, *some*, or *none*. Use *them* or *it* when possible and include *of* or *the* if necessary.

► 100% – sports – physical and – 20% – dangerous.
All sports are physical and some of them are dangerous. ....

► 80% – Hepworth's art – abstract and – 25% – difficult to understand
Most of Hepworth's art is abstract and some of it is difficult to understand. ....

1 80% – professional athletes – paid well and – 20% – very rich.
....

2 80% – ocean – very salty and – 0% – fresh water.
....

3 30% – current music – very good but – 20% – terrible.
....

4 75% – Indian food – spicy and – 15% – very spicy.
....

5 100% – my relatives – slim and – 0% – very tall.
....

6 75% – my friends – students but – 0% – very smart.
....

7 80% – Nepal – mountainous and – 0% – flat.
....

8 75% – the earth – is covered in water but – 10% – desert.
....

As/like; as if/as though

1 We use **as + noun:**

- to talk about someone's job or role:
  *She works **as an assistant** in a laboratory.*
  *He came to fame **as the main character** in a successful movie.*
- to talk about the function or use of something:
  *I lent him some money **as a favour**.*
  *You can use this sofa **as a bed**.*

2 We use **as** in phrases that refer to something that has already been stated or is already known:

As I told you last week, I'm going away tomorrow.
As you know, some friends are staying with me this weekend.

3 We use **as** after certain verbs for giving descriptions or talking about attitudes:

*She **described** her boss **as** a very unpleasant person.*
*I **regard** her **as** my best friend.*

4 We use **as** in the phrases **such as, the same as,** and **as usual:**

*Some sports, **such as** golf, don't interest me.* (= for example)
*I really like buildings **such as** this.* (= of the same type)
*His income is about **the same as** mine.*
***As usual,** she gave me some very good advice.*

5 We use **like + noun/pronoun** for comparing, with the meaning "similar to":

*He doesn't behave **like other people**.*
***Like most boys his age,** he causes trouble.*
*I wish I could sing **like you**.*

6 We use **like + noun/pronoun** with the meaning "in a similar way to":

*If you cook it **like this**, it always tastes better.*

7 We use **like + noun/pronoun** with the meaning "such as":

*Some people, **like my brother**, really love their jobs.*
*I really enjoy music **like this**.*

8 We use **look, sound, taste, feel + like + noun/pronoun** to talk about the appearance of someone/something or the impression something gives us:

*She doesn't **look like her sister** at all.*
*He **sounds like his father** when he speaks.*
*This **tastes like coffee**.*

9 We use **as if/as though + subject, verb,** etc. with the meaning "in a way that suggests ... ."

We use **as if/as though + subject** to describe how something seems:

*He talks **as if** he's an expert on the subject.* (= he isn't or may not really be an expert)
*She acted **as though** we had never met before.* (= but we had met before)

Practice

A Complete these sentences, taken from reviews of new songs, using *as* or *like*.

- This single sounds exactly like............ the band's previous one.

1 Right now, there is no one quite .... this singer on the music scene.
2 Many people regard her .... one of the best singers in Canada at the moment.
3 Although she looks .... a small and delicate girl, she has a very big voice.
4 .... everyone knows, this band shot to fame last year.
5 He describes this new song .... an experiment with a new style of music.
6 Bands .... this tend to be popular for only a short time.

B Complete the dialogues using *as* or *like*.

► A: What did you do before this job?
  B: I spent seven years as............ a university professor.

1 A: Are you coming to the party tonight?
  B: No, ... I told you before, I'm going somewhere else.

2 A: Do you like this show?
  B: No, it's .... all those reality TV shows. It's really boring.

3 A: I'm having trouble doing this job on the computer.
  B: That's because you shouldn't try to do it .... that. Look, I'll show you.

4 A: Let's stay at this hotel for the whole trip.
  B: Yes, we can use it .... a base for travelling around the region.

5 A: Did you enjoy the book I lent you?
  B: Yes, I don't usually enjoy novels .... that, but it was excellent.

6 A: Did you discuss the problem with William?
  B: Yes, and .... I thought, it was an easy one to solve.

7 A: What's your opinion of Ann?
  B: I get along with her most of the time, but sometimes she acts .... a child.

8 A: That was a horrible thing to say.
  B: Don't get upset. I only said it .... a joke.

C Complete these sentences describing people, using *as*, *like*, or *as if/as though*.

► Felicity behaves as if/as though..... she's more important than everyone else.

1 Sarah doesn't think .... other people; she has her own ideas.

2 .... most people know, Colin has not had an easy life.

3 Sabrina dresses .... the girls she sees in magazines.

4 Sotiris talks .... money is the only thing in life that matters.

5 .... all his friends, James is extremely interested in kayaking.

6 When he talks, Simon sounds .... someone who is not from this town.

7 .... a student, Ming works very hard and is very serious.

D Complete these sentences, using *as*, *like*, or *as if/as though*.

► He's a very good guitarist and he sounds like................. a professional when he plays.

1 People .... him really make me angry.

2 This doesn't taste .... anything I've eaten before.

3 He has been described .... the best goalie in the world.

4 .... usual, she arrived late for work.

5 Older people such .... my parents have different attitudes from mine.

6 Most people were shocked but she acted .... nothing important had happened.

7 You sound .... you've got a sore throat.

8 What you're telling me now is not the same .... what you told me yesterday.

Comparison: (not) as ... as

1 We use **as + adjective + as** (e.g. **as old as**) to say that two things or people are the same in some way:

*The chair is **as expensive as** the table.*
*You're **as old as** I (am).* (= We are the same age.)

Note that in spoken English, we often say **as me/as him/as her/as us/as them**, instead of **as I/as he/as she**, etc:
*She's as strong as **he** (is)./She's as strong as **him**.*
*I'm as fast as they are./I'm as fast as **them**.*

We use **not as ... as** to talk about a difference between two things or people:

*The two-star hotel **isn't as big as** the four-star hotel.*
*I'm **not as smart as** she is.* (= She is smarter than me.)

2 We can also use **as + adverb + as** (e.g. **as well as**):
*Jean cooks **as well as** Tom.* (= Jean and Tom are both good cooks.)
*He couldn't run **as quickly as** Maria.* (= Maria ran more quickly than him.)

3 We use **as many + plural noun + as** (e.g. **as many friends as**) to say that the numbers of two things are equal:
*Javier has got **as many friends as** Mei Ling.*

We use **not as many ... as** to say two things are not equal:
*I **don't** have **as many books as** you (do).*

4 We use **as much + uncountable noun + as** (e.g. **as much money as**) to compare two things. Uncountable nouns are words for things that we cannot count, and so they do not have a plural form (e.g. **money, work, luggage, traffic**):
*Helen earns **as much money as** Colin.*
*Jack doesn't do **as much work as** me/as I (do).*
*They aren't carrying **as much luggage as** us/ as we are.*

Practice

A Complete each sentence so that it means the same as the one above it. Use *as + adjective/adverb + as*.

► Canada is bigger than Mexico.
Mexico isn't as big as Canada .

1 The other students learn more quickly than I do.
I don't learn .... the other students.

2 You're very angry and I'm very angry also.
I'm .... you are.

3 The seats at the front are more expensive than the seats at the back.
The seats at the back aren't .... the seats at the front.

4 Central Park in New York is smaller than Stanley Park in Vancouver.
Central Park in New York isn't .... Stanley Park in Vancouver.

5 Her last movie was very good and her new movie is also very good.
Her new movie is .... her last movie.

6 The other students work harder than he does.
He doesn't work .... the other students.

B **Complete the sentences about each picture, using *as … as* and a word from the box. Use each word once.**

long	clean	fast	fresh	tall	big	~~cheap~~	strong	wide	full

►

1

2

3

4

5

6

7

8

9

► The carrots aren't *as cheap as*........ the cabbages.
1 The black car is going .... the grey car.
2 The soccer players aren't .... the basketball players.
3 Janet's hair is .... Kathy's hair.
4 The car on the left isn't .... the car on the right.
5 The flowers on the right aren't .... the flowers on the left.
6 The big glass isn't .... the little glass.
7 Jane is .... Matthew.
8 High Street isn't .... Main Street.
9 The black book is .... the grey book.

C **Join each pair of sentences in parentheses ( ), using *as much … as* or *as many … as*.**

► (I've got about 50 books. Jack's got about 100.)
I haven't got *as many books as*.. Jack has.
► (You've done a lot of work. I've done a lot of work also.)
I've done *as much work as*... you have.
1 (Abed earns a lot of money. Sheila only earns a little.)
Sheila doesn't earn .... Abed does.
2 (George has been to five countries. I've also been to five countries.)
I've been to .... George has.
3 (You've had five jobs. I've only had two.)
I haven't had .... you have.
4 (Tom has a lot of luggage. Sherida has a lot of luggage, too.)
Sherida has .... Tom has.
5 (Dani answered most of the questions. I only answered about half.)
I didn't answer .... Dani did.
6 (Ruth spent $50. I also spent $50.)
I spent .... Ruth did.

Too and enough

1 Look at this example:

*The case is **too heavy.** He can't carry it.*

We use **too** to mean "more than is good or suitable in the situation."

2 We can use **too** like this:

> **too** + ADJECTIVE:
> *I don't want to go out. I'm **too tired.***
>
> **too many** + PLURAL NOUN:
> *I couldn't find her at the concert because there were **too many people** there.*
>
> **too much** + UNCOUNTABLE NOUN:
> (e.g. **too much work/money/food/noise/salt/information/time/bread**)
> *Our teacher gives us **too much homework.***

3 We can use **too** with **to** + **infinitive** to explain why someone cannot do something:

*She's **too young to drive.*** (= She can't drive because she's too young.)

4 Now look at this example:

*This suitcase is **big enough.** I can put all my clothes into it. The small suitcase **isn't big enough.***

We use **enough** to mean "as much or as many as we need." We use **not … enough** to mean "less than we need."

5 We can use **enough** like this:

> ADJECTIVE + **enough:**
> *Is your room **warm enough?***
>
> **enough** + PLURAL NOUN:
> *I have **enough pancakes,** thanks.*
>
> **enough** + UNCOUNTABLE NOUN:
> *I can't talk to you now. I don't have **enough time.***

6 We can also use **not … enough** + **to** + **infinitive** to say why someone cannot do something:

*She **isn't old enough to drive.*** (= She can't drive because she isn't old enough.)

Practice

A **Complete the sentences using *too* or *enough* and the word in parentheses ( ).**

► I can't eat this soup because it's too hot.............. (hot).
► We couldn't buy the tickets because we didn't have enough money...... (money).
► We didn't buy the car because it wasn't big enough........... (big).
1 I couldn't see her because it was .... (dark).
2 I can't decide what to do because I don't have .... (information).
3 You can't change the situation now. It's .... (late).
4 Have you had .... (food), or would you like some more?
5 He did badly on the test because he was .... (nervous).
6 Slow down! You're driving .... (fast).
7 He shouldn't play on the team because he isn't .... (good).
8 I don't have .... (clothes). I need to buy some more.
9 Robert didn't go to work because he didn't feel .... (well).
10 I couldn't lift the suitcase because I wasn't .... (strong).
11 We didn't go swimming because the water was .... (cold).
12 Grace couldn't mail the package because she didn't have .... (stamps).

B **Complete the sentences using *too much*, *too many*, or *enough* and the word in parentheses ( ).**

► I'm not enjoying my job because they're giving me too much work.............. (work).
► Is your coffee sweet enough.............. (sweet)?
1 Shall we have another coffee? Do we have .... (time)?
2 I couldn't finish the exam because there were .... (questions).
3 We didn't go for a walk because it wasn't .... (warm).
4 I couldn't eat the food because there was .... (salt) in it.
5 Rosa passed the test because she answered .... (questions) correctly.
6 I didn't enjoy the party because there were .... (people) there.
7 Is that chair .... (comfortable) or would you like to sit here?
8 Gobi couldn't work because the others were making .... (noise).
9 We can't play that game because we don't have .... (players).
10 Shall I make some sandwiches? Have we got .... (bread)?
11 Her work isn't very good. She makes .... (mistakes).

C **Join each pair of sentences using *too* or *enough* with *to + infinitive* (e.g. *to do*, *to go*).**

► Clare couldn't sleep. She was too worried.
Clare was too worried to sleep..
► I can't go on vacation. I don't have enough money.
I don't have enough money to go on vacation...
1 I can't do any more work. I'm too tired.
....
2 Heidi won't pass the exam. She isn't smart enough.
....
3 Clive can't play basketball. He's too short.
....
4 His girlfriend couldn't go to the party. She was too sick.
....
5 David couldn't pay the bill. He didn't have enough money.
....
6 Shall we go to the beach? Is it hot enough?
....
7 I can't see you tonight. I'm too busy.
....
8 I don't want to go home. It's too early.
....
9 Chris couldn't fix the car. He didn't have enough tools.
....
10 I didn't visit all the museums. I didn't have enough time.
....

Adjectives: **-ed** or **-ing**

1 Compare **frightened** and **frightening:**

We can use adjectives that end with **-ed** to describe people's feelings:

SUBJECT
*Ann was very **frightened.***

The subject of the sentence (e.g. **Ann**) is the person who has the feeling.

We use an adjective that ends with **-ing** (e.g. frightening) to talk about a thing or person that makes us have a feeling:

SUBJECT
*The ghost was very **frightening.***

The subject of the sentence (e.g. **the ghost**) causes the feeling.

2 Here are some more examples to compare:

*We are all **surprised** by the news.* (= *We feel surprised.*)	*The news is **surprising.*** (= *The news makes us feel surprised.*)
*I was very **tired** at the end of the trip.* (= *I felt tired.*)	*The trip was very **tiring.**** (= *The trip made us feel tired.*)
*He was **excited** by the way the game ended.*	*The end of the game was **exciting.***
*I'm **interested** in your idea.*	*Your idea is **interesting.***
*The students were **bored** during the lesson.*	*The lesson was **boring.***
*Were you **disappointed** by the movie?*	*Was the movie **disappointing?***
*I wasn't nervous before the test; I was **relaxed.***	*I went for a **relaxing** walk.*
*The children were **entertained** by three clowns.*	*The clowns were very **entertaining.***
*Jack was totally **convinced** by Vlad's explanation*	*Vlad's explanation was totally **convincing.***

*Note that we can say:
*The trip was very **tiring.***
OR:
*It was a very **tiring trip.***

Practice

A **Choose the correct adjective in parentheses ( ) to write in the blank.**

► It was a terrible play and I was bored......... (bored/boring) from start to finish.
1 I'm very .... (excited/exciting) because I'm going to Paris tomorrow.
2 Are you .... (surprised/surprising) or were you expecting this news?
3 I'm reading a very .... (interested/interesting) book at the moment.
4 I've had a very .... (tired/tiring) day at work today and I want to go to bed.
5 Most people were .... (surprised/surprising) that he won the award.
6 I'm .... (bored/boring). Let's go out for a cup of coffee somewhere.
7 Visit our .... (excited/exciting) new store!
8 His speech was very long and very .... (bored/boring).

B Complete each sentence using the correct word from the box. Use each word once.

bored	interested	surprising	amusing	confused
boring	amused	confusing	surprised	~~interesting~~

► Your idea is very *interesting*... Tell me more about it.
1 He told me a very .... story. I laughed and laughed.
2 This is a very .... book. Nothing happens in it.
3 She's .... in politics and often talks about it.
4 The map was .... and I got lost.
5 She was .... because she had nothing to do all day.
6 Everyone else thought it was funny, but she wasn't ....
7 Could you repeat that, please? I'm a bit .... because it was very complicated.
8 It is .... that she failed the test, because she's a good student.
9 Everyone was .... by the sudden noise.

C Complete the dialogue using the words from the box.

bored	boring	confusing	convinced	convincing	disappointed	~~entertained~~
entertaining	frightened	interesting	relaxed	surprised	surprising	

Craig: What sort of movies do you like?
Liz: When I go to the theatre, I like to be (►) *entertained*.................. .
Craig: And what sort of movies do you find (1)................................ ?
Liz: Well, I like movies that tell a good (2)................................ story. And I mean a story that you can follow, not the sort that goes backwards and forwards in time. I find those very (3)................................ . And I'm (4)................................ . when I watch a horror film. I usually close my eyes when the scary part starts.
Craig: Yes, but if the story is too simple, surely you get (5)................................ because you know exactly what's going to happen.
Liz: I don't mean that. If something is intelligible, it's not necessarily (6)................................ . Often good stories have (7)................................ events or endings – things that you can't possibly know at the beginning.
Craig: For me, the most important thing is that the actors must be (8)................................ so that you really believe that they are the person they are pretending to be.
Liz: If that's true, I imagine that you are (9)................................ most of the time because, well, for example, Will Smith is always Will Smith. I'm never (10)................................ that he's somebody else.
Craig: Yes, but it's often not important in his movies because they're escapist – if you're feeling tense about work or something, you have a good laugh and you come out feeling (11)................................ and happy with the world.
Liz: I'm (12)................................ that you like his movies. Although the special effects are good, the story is always very simple.
Craig: He's not my favourite, but his movies are not bad.

Adverbs: place, direction, sequence

1 We use **here** with the meaning "in or to this place/the place where the speaker is":

*I've been living **here** for three years.*
*Come **here**, I want to speak to you.*

We use **there** with the meaning "in or to that place/another place, away from where the speaker is":

*Stay **there**. I'll get you.*
*Go and stand **there**. I'll take a picture of you.*

We also use **there** with the meaning "in or to a place previously mentioned":

*I lived in the Northwest Territories for a year and I made a lot of friends while I was **there**.*

We often use **over here** and **over there** when we are speaking informally:

*Come **over here** and sit down.*

2 Some common adverbs describing a place or a movement in a particular direction are:

abroad (= in/to another country), **ahead, away, back, downstairs/upstairs, in/out, inside/outside** (= in or out of a building), **nearby, forward/backward(s)/sideways**

*Lan is **abroad** but she's coming back soon.*
*She ran **downstairs** and opened the front door.*
*He walked **out**, saying that he couldn't stay.*
*The line slowly moved **forward**.*

Notice that we use **out** with the meaning "not at home/work etc. for part of a day or a day" and **away** with the meaning "not at home/work etc. for more than a day":

*Mr. Rampaul is **out** at the moment. He'll be back at around twelve o'clock.*
*Mr. Rampaul is **away** this week. He's at a three-day conference.*

3 We often use these adverbial phrases when giving someone directions to a place:

straight ahead, turn left/right, on the left/right (to say where something is), **to the left/right** (for movement), **as far as**

*Go **straight ahead**. When you get to the intersection, **turn right**. The first road **on the left** is the one you want.*

4 When we talk about a number of actions or events that happen one after the other, we can indicate the order with these adverbs and adverbial phrases:

first(ly)/first of all, second(ly), third(ly), etc, last(ly), finally

Instead of using **secondly**, **thirdly**, etc., we often use these adverbs and adverbial phrases to link actions or events in a sequence:

then, next, afterwards, after that

*To make this dish, **first** you dice some tomatoes, **then** you get some garlic ...*
***First of all** I went to St. John's, **after that** I spent some time in Halifax, **then** I travelled around New Brunswick and **finally** I went to Prince Edward Island.*

Practice

A Complete the sentences with the correct adverb in parentheses ( ).

► Joan lived abroad....... (abroad/away) for several years, mostly in India.
1 We had to wait .... (out/outside) until the museum opened.
2 I'm going .... (out/away) now and I'll be back in about an hour.
3 Fortunately there was a hospital .... (nearby/sideways).
4 I went .... (upstair/upstairs) and looked for the bathroom.
5 The traffic slowly moved .... (forward/out).
6 We're going .... (out/away) for the weekend.
7 Jesse has gone .... (out/away) until the end of the week.
8 Would you like to live .... (away/abroad)?

B **Complete the directions from the bus station to Matt's house, using these adverbial phrases:**

on the right	turn left	straight ahead	turn right	~~turn right~~

► As you leave the station, turn right .

1 .... at the first intersection.

2 Go .... until you reach the traffic lights.

3 .... onto my road.

4 You'll find my house ....

C **Look at this sequence of events and put them in the correct order. Link the events, using suitable adverbs or adverbial phrases. More than one answer is possible in each blank.**

> How I found an apartment to rent:
>
> I agreed with the landlord that I would rent it.
> I made a list of apartments I could afford.
> I signed the lease.
> I went to see some of the apartments.
> ~~I looked through the ads in the local newspaper.~~
> I moved into the apartment.
> I paid the last month's rent as a deposit.
> I decided which apartment to rent.

► First of all/First(ly), I looked through the ads in the local newspaper.

1 ....

2 ....

3 ....

4 ....

5 ....

6 ....

7 ....

Adverb + adjective; noun + noun; etc.

1

It was cold.

It was very cold.

We can use an adverb (e.g. **very**) before an adjective (e.g. **cold**) to make the adjective stronger. Some common adverbs we use in this way are:

very **extremely** **really**

*We were **very tired** after the trip.*
*I felt **extremely nervous** before the test.*
*I'm **really angry** with you.* (= very angry)

We can also make an adjective weaker with these adverbs:

fairly **somewhat**

*Our car is **fairly old**.* (= It's old, but it isn't very old.)
*It was **somewhat late** when we finally arrived.* (= It was late but not very late.)

2 When we use two adjectives together, we order them like this:

► We use "opinion" adjectives (e.g. **wonderful, nice, pleasant, strange**) before any other adjective (e.g. **new**):

	OPINION	
a	*wonderful*	new product
a	*lovely*	warm day
a	*beautiful*	little house
a	*horrible*	green shirt

► We use "size" adjectives (e.g. **big, tall**) before an adjective that gives other information – for example, its age (**new, old**), its colour, its shape (**thin, round**):

	SIZE	
a	*big*	new building
a	*small*	red mark
a	*huge*	black cloud
a	*large*	round rock

3 We can use two nouns together. The first noun is like an adjective and gives information about the second noun:

	NOUN	+ NOUN
a	*cardboard*	*box*
a	*wind*	*turbine*
a	*cheque*	*book*
an	*alarm*	*clock*

Practice

A Complete these sentences using *really* or *fairly*.

► The film was really......... good. I enjoyed it a lot.
1 It's .... cold outside, but not very cold.
2 It isn't a wonderful book, but it's .... good.
3 The tickets were .... expensive – they cost much more than I expected.
4 This show is .... popular in my country; millions of people watch it.
5 He's .... good at his job, but he sometimes makes bad mistakes.
6 The meal was .... nice, but it wasn't great.
7 It's .... dangerous to drive so fast in such terrible weather conditions.
8 I'm not a very good rugby player, but I am .... good.
9 They're all .... intelligent students, and they will all pass the tests easily.
10 The company that I work for is .... big, but it's not enormous.

B Write these words in the correct order.

► (a – town – beautiful – little) a beautiful little town

1 (a – day – pleasant – sunny) ....

2 (a – smile – big – nice) ....

3 (a – large – coffee – black) ....

4 (a – old – coat – dirty) ....

5 (a – large – building – white) ....

6 (a – moose – big – brown) ....

7 (a – woman – thin – tall) ....

8 (a – small – car – blue) ....

9 (a – story – little – strange) ....

C Match the words in box A and box B to describe what you can see in each picture.

A			B		
~~table~~	tennis	paper	cup	court	pot
photo	door	soup	handle	sign	hanger
street	flight	stereo	system	bowl	~~lamp~~
coat	coffee	phone	book	attendant	album

► a table lamp

1 ....

2 ....

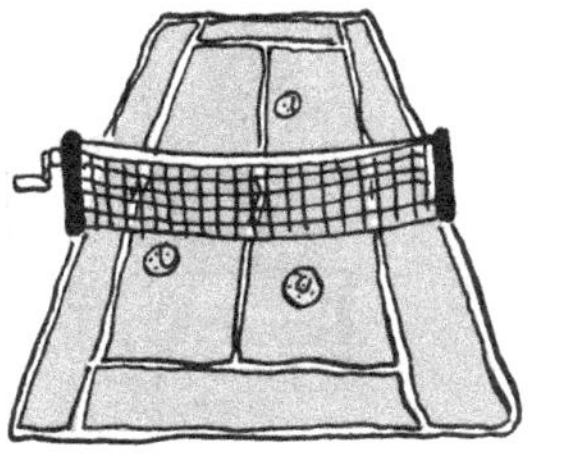

3 ....

4 ....

5 ....

6 ....

7 ....

8 ....

9 ....

10 ....

11 ....

Prepositions of place and movement

1 **In**, **on**, and **at** are used to talk about places:

- We use **in** with enclosed spaces (e.g. rooms, buildings) and limited areas (e.g. cities, provinces, countries, continents):
  in *my pocket* ***in*** *her car* ***in*** *Germany*
- We use **on** with surfaces (e.g. walls, floors, shelves) and lines (e.g. streets, coasts, the equator):
  on *the grass* ***on*** *the west coast*
  on *Bay Street* ***on*** *the third floor*
- We use **at** with a point (e.g. **at** the bus stop), and **at** with a building, when we mean either inside or outside:
  A: *Let's meet* ***at*** *the arena.*
  B: *OK. Shall we meet* ***in*** *the arena itself or* ***on*** *the sidewalk outside?*

2 Look at the illustration and read the sentences:

There is a bank ***in*** *the town.*
There are people ***outside*** *the theatre.*
The people are ***on*** *the sidewalk.*
There is a clock ***above*** *the theatre entrance.*
The theatre entrance is ***under*** *the clock.*
The bank is ***next to/beside*** *the theatre.*
The bank is ***between*** *the theatre and the café.*
There is a hill ***behind*** *the town.*
The car is ***in front of*** *the bank.*

3 **Into**, **onto**, and **to** are used to talk about movement:
We moved the chairs ***into*** *my bedroom.*
The actor ran ***onto*** *the stage.*
They walked ***to*** *the next town.*
The opposites are **out of**, **off**, and **from**:
We moved the chairs ***out of*** *my bedroom.*
The actor ran ***off*** *the stage.*
We drove ***from*** *Red Deer to Calgary.*
Here are other prepositions of movement:
They ran ***across*** *the field to the road.*
Jim cycled ***along*** *the road to the next town.*
I walked ***up*** *the hill and ran* ***down*** *the other side.*
The bus went ***past*** *the bus stop without stopping.*
The train goes ***through*** *three tunnels.*

Practice

A The sentences below describe the picture. Look at the picture and change any incorrect underlined words. Check (✓) the underlined words which are correct.

- ► There is a TV under ...on... the table.
- ► There is a dog on ...✓... the floor.
- 1 The table is in front of .... the picture.
- 2 There is a book under .... the table.
- 3 The cat is behind .... the TV.
- 4 There is a dog under .... the table.
- 5 The bird is on .... the cage.
- 6 The flowers are in .... the vase.
- 7 The keys are between .... the vase and the cat.
- 8 There is a book in front of .... the vase.

B Write *in*, *on*, or *at* in the blanks.

► Peter lives in........ Turkey.
1 Let's meet .... your house.
2 He works .... the Prairie Oil Company .... Alberta.
3 Is the store .... Victoria Street?
4 I live in an apartment .... the fifth floor.
5 Peru is .... South America.
6 They are waiting .... the restaurant.

C Write the words from the box in the blanks.

into (x3)	onto (x2)	~~to~~	out of	off

► The parade started in the park. From there we marched to.............. the town hall.
1 The tiger escaped from its cage and jumped .... the lake. It took a long time to get it .... the lake and back .... its cage.
2 Stupidly, Simon drove his car .... the beach and then he couldn't move it, because the wheels sank .... the sand. In the end, he needed eight people to push it .... the beach and back .... the road.

D Look at this picture of a town showing the route for a race.

Now fill in the blanks using the words from the box.

across	along	~~at~~	down	in front of	past	from	under	through	up

The race starts (►) at.............. the town hall. The runners go away (1)................ the town hall and they run (2)................ the main square to the river. Then they run over New Bridge and they go (3)................ the road beside the river for about 200 metres. They go (4)................ the theatre and (5)................ Castle Hill. They turn right (6)................ the castle, and they go (7)................ Steep Hill. Then they go (8)................ the tunnel (9)................ the river, and they finish at the station.

In; **with**; preposition + **-ing**

1 We can use **in** to describe what somebody is wearing:

*Tanya is the woman **in** the red dress.*
*I went to the interview **in** my new suit.*
*It was a sunny day, and everyone was **in** summer clothes.*
*Are you allowed to go to work **in** jeans?*
*We saw some Mounties **in** uniform.*

2 We can use **with** to describe a part of somebody's body:

*A small boy **with** red hair came into the store.*
*Our teacher is a tall man **with** a beard.*
*Lisa is a pretty girl **with** blue eyes.*
*Jack was talking to a man **with** a big nose.*

We can also use **with** to describe animals:

*A beaver is an animal **with** small ears and a large tail.*

3 We can use **with** to talk about a part of something:

*They live in a white house **with** a flat roof.*
*I bought a shirt **with** red stripes.*
*I used the pot **with** the wooden handle.*
*He has a stereo **with** very big speakers.*

4 We can use **with** before something (for example, a tool) that we use in order to do something:

*You brush your teeth **with** a toothbrush.*
*You open a can **with** a can opener.*
*I cleaned the table **with** a cloth.*
*Please eat **with** your knife and fork.*

5 We use **by** + **-ing** (e.g. **by doing**) to describe how we do or did something:

*She learned French **by speaking** with her grandparents.*
*You start a car **by turning** the key.*
*She became successful in business **by working** very hard.*
*The prisoners escaped **by climbing** over a wall.*

We use **without** + **-ing** (e.g. **without doing**) to say that a particular action is not done or was not done:

*She passed the test **without doing** a lot of work.*
*They left **without waiting** for me.*
*He did the work **without making** any mistakes.*

Practice

A Write the correct prepositions. Use *in* or *with*.

► A young man with.......... a moustache was driving the car.
1 He showed me a picture of a woman .... brown eyes.
2 We live in a house .... a green door.
3 A lot of businessmen .... suits were on the subway.
4 There was a plant .... big green leaves in the corner of the room.
5 Jacob was walking down the street with a woman .... a black coat.
6 Look at that bear .... those enormous paws!
7 One of the children was a girl .... long, dark hair.
8 A man .... a hat came into the café.
9 Police officers .... uniform were standing at the entrance to the building.
10 She decided to discuss the problem .... her Nation's council.
11 We booked a hotel room .... two beds.
12 It was cold, so I went out .... mittens and a toque.
13 We bought a television .... a big screen.
14 He arrived for the meeting .... a grey jacket.

B **Match each phrase in the first column with a phrase from the second column and add the appropriate preposition.**

► You must speak to the woman
1 A giraffe is an animal
2 I want a shirt
3 She brushes her teeth
4 They live in a house
5 I like my coffee
6 He's clearing the snow
7 She painted the kitchen
8 You should always cut meat
9 They got into the house
10 The officers do all their exercises
11 She has a car
12 He dried his hair
13 You can't make an omelette
14 Some women prefer men

a a sharp knife.
b a towel.
c a shovel.
d cream and sugar.
e beards.
f a brush.
g the green skirt.
h breaking a window.
i a chimney.
j uniform.
k toothpaste.
l a very long neck.
m a round collar.
n breaking eggs.
o a sun roof.

►	in (g)	1	....	2	....	3	....	4	....
5	....	6	....	7	....	8	....	9	....
10	....	11	....	12	....	13	....	14	....

C **Rewrite each of the following using *by* or *without*.**

► She sat in the corner. She didn't say anything.
She sat in the corner without saying anything.

► He opened the door. He turned the key.
He opened the door by turning the key.

1 He fixed the car. He changed some of the parts.
....

2 She answered the question but she didn't read it carefully.
....

3 He left. He didn't say thank you.
....

4 She got the money because she sold her car.
....

5 I deleted the email. I didn't read it.
....

6 We worked all day and we didn't eat anything.
....

7 He lost weight. He went on a strict diet.
....

8 I went out, but I didn't lock the door.
....

And, but, so, both ... and, either, etc.

1 We use **and** and **both ... and** to link two similar ideas in one sentence:

She is tired. She is hungry.

*She is tired **and** hungry.*
*She is **both** tired **and** hungry.*

*We found **both** our tickets **and** our money.*

2 We use **but** to contrast two different ideas:
He swims. He doesn't play tennis.
*He swims, **but** he doesn't play tennis.*
*I live in Kitchener, **but** I work in Toronto.*

3 We use **so** to talk about the result of something; it links two actions (= and therefore ...)

SITUATION: *I'm tired.* RESULT: *I'm going to bed.*

*I'm tired, **so** I'm going to bed.*
*They were late, **so** they missed the train.*

4 We use **or** and **either ... or** to talk about two possibilities:

POSSIBILITY A: *She's Korean.* POSSIBILITY B: *She's Japanese.*

*She's Korean **or** Japanese.*
*She's **either** Korean **or** Japanese.*
*That man is **either** a singer **or** an actor.*
*I never work all day. I work **either** in the morning **or** in the afternoon.*

5 We use **neither ... nor** to put two negative statements together:

Didier didn't come. *Joan didn't come.*

***Neither** Didier **nor** Joan came.*

The verb form (**came**) is positive, because **neither ... nor** makes the sentence negative:
NOT ~~*Neither Didier nor Joan didn't come.*~~

6 We can also use **both**, **either**, and **neither** like this:

both / either / neither } of { the / my / his / these } PLURAL NOUN

PLURAL VERB
***Both of these suitcases** are heavy.*
*I haven't seen **either of the movies.***

SINGULAR OR PLURAL VERB
***Neither of his sisters** was/were there.*

We can also say:

both/either/neither + of + them/us

*He has two cars, but **neither of them** works.*

Practice

A Write *but* or *so* in the blanks.

► The movie was very long, but..... it was interesting.
so..... we got home late.

1 The sun is shining, ... it's very windy.
.... I'm going for a walk.

2 I don't like my job, ... I'm going to look for a new one.
.... it pays well.

3 Matthew wants to visit South America, ... he doesn't have money for the trip.
.... he's taking Spanish lessons.

4 We saw a movie on Friday, ... we'll probably stay in on Saturday night.
.... it wasn't very good.

5 They were going to a baseball game, ... they put on sunscreen.
.... it began to rain.

6 She hasn't started studying for her test yet, ... she still has a few days.
.... she probably won't do well.

B Combine these sentences using *both ... and*.

► Jane owns a store. She owns a restaurant. *Jane owns both a store and a restaurant.*

1 Rebecca plays hockey. She plays softball. ....

2 This book is long. It is boring. ....

3 I am going to New York this summer.
I am going to Boston this summer. ....

4 My niece is a very active child.
My nephew is a very active child. ....

C Now combine these sentences using *either ... or*.

► POSSIBILITY A: She's at the office. POSSIBILITY B: She's at the airport.
She's either at the office or at the airport.

1 POSSIBILITY A: Maria is going to study law. POSSIBILITY B: Maria is going to study medicine.
....

2 POSSIBILITY A: You have the flu. POSSIBILITY B: You have a cold.
....

3 POSSIBILITY A: He is sick. POSSIBILITY B: He is on vacation.
....

4 POSSIBILITY A: I am going skiing at Banff. POSSIBILITY B: I am going skiing at Tremblant.
....

D Now combine these sentences using *neither ... nor*.

► Chris didn't have time to take a vacation. Sheila didn't have time to take a vacation.
Neither Chris nor Sheila had time to take a vacation.

1 My mom has never been to Europe. My dad has never been to Europe.
....

2 The beach isn't clean. The lake isn't clean.
....

3 Annie isn't happy about the decision. Joe isn't happy about the decision.
....

4 The kids didn't like the restaurant. The adults didn't like the restaurant.
....

E Complete the sentences with *both/either/neither* + *of* + *us/them* (e.g. *neither of us*).

► I went to the concert with Mary, but *neither of us*........ enjoyed it very much because it was very boring.

1 Danny and I want to play soccer this summer but not with a competitive team because .... is very good.

2 I like the red dress and the blue dress. .... would be good for the party.

3 We could only get one ticket for the game, but .... want to go. If we can't go together, then .... will go.

4 I watched two movies this weekend and enjoyed .... I would definitely recommend them.

5 Emily was accepted at two excellent universities. Because .... are great schools, she could choose .... and be happy with her choice.

6 We cancelled our kids' piano lessons because .... was enjoying the lessons.

Relative clauses

1 In informal English, in defining relative clauses, when **who, that,** or **which** is the object of the verb, it can be omitted:

The name of the woman I interviewed was Mrs. Norris.
The car they bought was very expensive.

Notice that there is no pronoun in the relative clause:

The name of the woman I interviewed ~~her~~ was Mrs. Norris.
The car they bought ~~it~~ was very expensive.

2 When the verb has a preposition, in formal English the preposition goes with **whom** or **which**:

*That is the young man **to whom** I spoke.*
*The job **for which** she's applied is in Lethbridge.*

Informally, we can omit the relative word and then the preposition goes at the end of the relative clause:

*That is the young man I spoke **to**.*
*The job she's applied **for** is in Lethbridge.*

3 Informally, we often omit the relative word **when** after **day**, **year**, etc.:

*That was the **year** I finished university.*

We often omit the relative word **where** after **place**, **somewhere**, etc.:

*Do you know **a place / somewhere** we can get a good sandwich?*

We often omit the relative word **why** after **reason**:

*The real **reason** she came was to speak to my father.*

We often omit a relative expression after **way**:

*That's the **way** they greet each other in Quebec.*

Practice

A In the following sentences, cross out the words that are not possible or not necessary. If there are no such words, mark the sentence with a check (✓).

► The first book ~~which~~ he wrote ~~it~~ was *Subconscious Selling.* ....
► This is the boy who broke the window. ✓.......
1 Do you know the woman that my father's talking to? ....
2 They're going to close the factories that they make too much smog. ....
3 People who live in small apartments shouldn't have dogs. ....
4 An animal that comes out at night must have good eyes. ....
5 The canoe that my cousins paddled in it was overturned by a wave. ....
6 An amphibian is an animal that can live on land or in water. ....
7 People who are from Labrador are called Labradorians. ....

B In the following, if a sentence is incomplete, indicate where a word is necessary and write the word at the end. If the sentence is correct, mark it with a check (✓).

► Is there a store near here sells stamps?
Is there a store near here⁁sells stamps? that....................
► Mrs. Thomas is the teacher my sister likes best. ✓......................
1 Is this the bus goes to Red Deer? ....
2 The woman was talking to our class was wearing a blue shirt. ....
3 There's a great place we can go camping near here. ....
4 That was the day I learned to paddle a canoe. ....
5 Do you know anyone plays basketball? ....

6 This is the cake tastes like lemon. ....
7 I found the person I needed to speak to. ....

C In each case, combine the two sentences into one. Write *who*, *that*, *which*, or *where* only if it is necessary.

▶ I lent you a book. Have you read it?
Have you read the book I lent you ....?
▶ My mother works in a factory. It makes parts for cars.
The factory where my mother works .... makes parts for cars.
1 Will acted in a play. It was very good.
The play .... was very good.
2 This is the new clothing line. Ellissa designed it.
This is the new clothing line ....
3 This is Michelle. She makes the decisions about new employees.
Michelle is the one .... about new employees.
4 Sonia works in a factory. The factory produces microchips.
Sonia works in a factory ....
5 David has a son. His son plays soccer.
David has a son ....

D Karim and Lily are on a camping trip. Complete the conversation with the expressions from the box and include *that* if it is necessary.

I asked you to buy at the grocery store	we use at home for lighting candles
were in the garage	I baked myself
we'll have to drive to the nearest town	fits in my backpack
~~has a rain cover~~	will light even if they get wet
we could go fishing for food	keeps the bears away

Lily: We should set up our tent. Did you bring the one (▶) that has a rain cover.............. ? It's starting to rain.

Karim: No, I brought the small one (1).. . It's much lighter.

Lily: Did you bring the matches (2).. ? We'll need them to start our campfire.

Karim: No, I brought the ones (3)... . They've always worked well. Now where is the spray (4)... ? I thought I put it in my backpack.

Lily: I took it out to make room for our food. See? I made egg salad sandwiches on the bread (5)... .

Karim: Did you bring the other food (6)... ? We're camping for three nights!

Lily: No, I thought (7)... .

Karim: Did you bring the fishing poles (8)... ?

Lily: I forgot. I guess (9)... to buy some supplies.

Review test

Choose the right answer (a, b, c, d) and write a, b, c, or d, as in the example. The correct answers are on page 98.

Russia is the .....a..... country in the world.
a largest b larger c most large d most largest

Verbs and tenses

1 I .... in Nunavut.
a no live b don't live c live not d doesn't live

2 Where are your cousins? .... in the kitchen.
a They're siting b They sitting c There sitting d They're sitting

3 It's very cloudy today and ....
a it's raining b it rains c its raining d it raining

4 Edwin .... yesterday.
a didn't work b worked not c don't worked d didn't worked

5 What .... doing at noon yesterday?
a Karla were b Karla was c did Karla d was Karla

6 Have you .... to Peru?
a ever been b ever gone c been ever d gone ever

7 Mr. Persaud hasn't .... He should be here soon.
a arrived just b already arrived c arrived already d arrived yet

8 Bryan and Vanessa .... to Charlottetown last month.
a have moved b moved c did moved d has moved

9 She .... to Regina three times already this month.
a went b has gone c has been d was going

10 Raymond has .... here since 2009.
a being worked b working c been working d been worked

11 When we arrived, the train .... the station.
a already left b had already left c had left already d has left already

12 My parents .... visit us next weekend.
a will to b going to c are going to d are going

13 Tomorrow we can go for a hike if the weather .... good.
a is being b will be c would be d is

14 We can start as soon as they ....
a arrive | b are arriving | c will arrive | d are going to arrive

15 Jack doesn't speak French and ....
a Jill doesn't neither | b Jill neither | c neither Jill | d neither does Jill

16 What time did they arrive .... the airport?
a at | b in | c on | d to

17 She learned French .... listening to Radio-Canada.
a by | b for | c on | d with

18 We're going to .... some shopping.
a make | b get | c do | d have

Sentences and questions

19 Tina was hungry so I made ....
a a sandwich to her | b her a sandwich
c for her a sandwich | d to her a sandwich

20 How do you know? .... you?
a Who did tell | b Who have told | c Who told | d Who did told

21 How .... is the walk? More than fifteen minutes?
a often | b far | c much | d long

22 Rashida works at the museum, ...
a isn't it? | b isn't she? | c don't she? | d doesn't she?

Modals and other verbs

23 You .... buy a ticket before boarding the bus.
a might | b must | c might to | d must to

24 .... go to the grocery store after work.
a I've got to | b I've get to | c I was getting to | d I have got

25 In my opinion, you .... smoke so much.
a shouldn't to | b shouldn't | c needn't | d don't have to

26 Excuse me. .... you help me?
a Could | b May | c Shall | d Do

Passive

27 Research in Motion .... a pair of men in Waterloo.
a is started for | b is started by | c was started by | d was started for

Infinitives and -ing forms

28 When you've .... , I'll tell you what I think.
a stopped talking b stopped to talk
c been stopping talking d been stopped to talk

29 The story was very sad. It .... cry.
a made us to b made us c let us d let us to

30 The teacher .... go home early.
a wanted that we b made us to c decided us to d let us

Reported speech

31 Vera .... she lived in a small apartment.
a said me b said to me c told d told me

Articles, nouns, pronouns, etc.

32 Are you a vegetarian? ~ Yes, I never eat ....
a meat b the meat c some meat d a meat

33 .... is my favourite art.
a A music b The music c Music d Some music

34 Your children are very good. They always help .... a lot.
a each other b themselves c them d each the other

35 I want to check the meaning of these words. Can you .... ?
a get the dictionary for me b give to me the dictionary
c get the dictionary to me d give the dictionary for me

36 I don't know .... near here to have lunch.
a anything b something c anywhere d something

37 They've got two children. One is a doctor and .... is a teacher.
a the other b another c other d one other

38 He didn't see all of those movies, but he saw ....
a most them b most of it c them most d most of them

39 She described the thief .... a tall, bearded man.
a like b such as c as d as though

Adjectives and adverbs

40 Fredericton isn't .... Vancouver.
a big as b as big as c as big that d so big that

41 Sara is only 15. She isn't .... drive a car.
a enough old to b enough old for c old enough for d old enough to

42 We thought the book was ....
a very bored b much boring c very boring d much bored

43 Turn left at the gas station then go .... until you get to the school.
a ahead b straight ahead c on ahead d on straight

44 The way she said that made me ....
a extreme angrily b angrily extreme c extremely angry d angry extremely

Prepositions

45 After 25 minutes, take the potatoes .... the oven.
a out from b out of c from of d from out

46 I think we can meet .... the bus stop.
a on b at c in d behind

47 The train has to go .... three tunnels.
a across b along c through d under

48 Sven is over there – he's the one ....
a in the blonde hair b with the blonde hair
c in blonde hair d blonde haired

Building sentences

49 Claudio neither came .... sent a message.
a or b neither c nor d either

50 The team .... scored the most goals won the competition.
a , which b , that c that d which it

51 Do you know those boys .... are talking to Mackenzie?
a which b that they c who d who's

52 We saw that woman .... was on TV.
a the son of her b whose son c that the son d that the son

Appendix 1: Nouns

1 Plural nouns

1 We usually add **-s** to a noun to form the plural:

a book	→	*some **books***
one kilogram	→	*ten **kilograms***
radio	→	***radios***
loonie	→	***loonies***
canoe	→	***canoes***
tire	→	***tires***

2 After **-s**, **-ss**, **-sh**, **-ch**, and **-x** we add **-es**:

bus	→	***buses***	*dress*	→	***dresses***
glass	→	***glasses***	*dish*	→	***dishes***
wish	→	***wishes***	*beach*	→	***beaches***
watch	→	***watches***	*box*	→	***boxes***

3 When a noun ends in a consonant* + **-y**, the **y** changes to **-ies**:

city	→	***cities***	*family*	→	***families***
penny	→	***pennies***	*story*	→	***stories***

We do not change **y** after a vowel*:

day	→	***days***	*alley*	→	***alleys***

4 Nouns ending in **-f** or **-fe** have the plural **-ves**:

leaf	→	***leaves***	*life*	→	***lives***
shelf	→	***shelves***	*thief*	→	***thieves***

5 A few nouns ending in **-o** have **-es**:

potato	→	***potatoes***
tomato	→	***tomatoes***
hero	→	***heroes***

But most have **-s**:

photos	*pianos*	*radios*
stereos	*studios*	*zoos*

6 Some nouns have irregular plurals:

man	→	***men***	*woman*	→	***women***
child	→	***children***	*foot*	→	***feet***
mouse	→	***mice***	*sheep*	→	***sheep***
fish	→	***fish***	*person*	→	***people***
tooth	→	***teeth***	*moose*	→	***moose***

2 Uncountable nouns

1 Here is a list of common uncountable nouns:

ice	*water*	*rain*	*snow*
heat	*noise*	*cotton*	*glass*
gas	*money*	*luggage*	*information*
work	*homework*	*advice*	*news*
milk	*butter*	*bread*	*cheese*
tea	*coffee*	*sugar*	*meat*
jam	*toast*		

2 Uncountable nouns do not have a plural form:
heat (NOT ~~*heats*~~) *butter* (NOT ~~*butters*~~)

3 We do not use ~~**a/an**~~ with uncountable nouns, but we can use **some/any**, **the**, **much** (NOT ~~**many**~~), **such** and **my/your/his**, etc.:

*I always have **toast** and **jam** for breakfast.*
*I'd like **some coffee**, please.*
*Look at **the snow** outside.*
*How **much luggage** do you have?*
*We've had **such** wonderful **news**.*

4 Some nouns can be countable or uncountable:

*I heard **a noise** from downstairs.* (countable)
*I can't sleep. The neighbours are making **so much noise**.* (uncountable)

* Consonants: b c d f g h j k l m n p q r s t v w x y z
Vowels: a e i o u
Syllables: |***hit***| = 1 syllable, |***vi***|***sit***| = 2 syllables, |***re***|***mem***|***ber***| = 3 syllables

Appendix 2: Regular verbs

1 Simple Present

1 Add an -s to make the **he/she/it** form of most Simple Present verbs:

I/you/we/they	**he/she/it**
leave	*leaves*
make	*makes*
say	*says*
work	*works*

2 After -ss, -sh, -ch, -o, or -x (e.g. ***finish***, ***go***), we add **-es**:

I/you/we/they	**he/she/it**
catch	*catches*
finish	*finishes*
pass	*passes*
teach	*teaches*
do	*does*
go	*goes*
mix	*mixes*

3 When a verb ends in a consonant* + -y, the **y** changes to **-ies**:

I/you/we/they	**he/she/it**
fly	*flies*
try	*tries*
carry	*carries*
study	*studies*

2 The -ing form

1 For most verbs we add **-ing**:
ask → *asking* *go* → *going*

2 For verbs ending with a consonant + **-e**, we normally leave out **e** when we add **-ing**:
hope → *hoping* *live* → *living*
take → *taking*
But we keep a double **e** before **-ing**:
see → *seeing* *agree* → *agreeing*

3 When a verb ends in **-ie**, it changes to **y** when we add **-ing**:
die → *dying* *lie* → *lying*
But **y** does not change:
hurry → *hurrying*

4 When a word ends with one vowel* and one consonant (e.g. ***run***, ***swim***, ***jog***), we double the final consonant:
get → *getting* *jog* → *jogging*
run → *running* *swim* → *swimming*
But note that we do not double the consonant:
- when it is **y**, **w**, or **x** (e.g. ***stay***)
  buy → *buying* *draw* → *drawing*
  wax → *waxing* *stay* → *staying*
- when the final syllable* is not stressed
  listen → *listening* *visit* → *visiting*
  wonder → *wondering*

Note, however, that in Canadian English **l** is usually doubled, even if the syllable is unstressed (e.g. ***travel***):
cancel → *cancelling* *travel* → *travelling*

3 The past tense and past participles

1 Most verbs have **-ed** in the past tense; most past participles also end in **-ed**:

INFINITIVE	PAST TENSE	PAST/PASSIVE PARTICIPLE
happen	*happened*	*happened*
work	*worked*	*worked*

2 If the verb ends in **-e**, we add **d**:
live → *lived* *vote* → *voted*

3 When a verb ends in a consonant + -y, the **y** changes to **-ied**:
study → *studied* *try* → *tried*

4 When a word ends with one vowel and one consonant (e.g. ***stop***), we double the final consonant:
grab → *grabbed* *plan* → *planned*
stop → *stopped*
But note that we do not double the consonant:
- when it is **y**, **w**, or **x** (e.g. ***enjoy***)
  allow → *allowed* *enjoy* → *enjoyed*
- when the final syllable is not stressed
  open → *opened* *listen* → *listened*
  discover → *discovered*

Note, however, that in Canadian English **l** is usually doubled, even if the syllable is unstressed (e.g. ***travel***):
cancel → *cancelled* *travel* → *travelled*

* Consonants: b c d f g h j k l m n p q r s t v w x y z
Vowels: a e i o u
Syllables: |*hit*| = 1 syllable, |*vi*|*sit*| = 2 syllables, |*re*|*mem*|*ber*| = 3 syllables

Appendix 3: Irregular verbs

INFINITIVE	PAST TENSE	PAST/PASSIVE PARTICIPLE
be	was/were	been
beat	beat	beaten
become	became	become
begin	began	begun
blow	blew	blown
break	broke	broken
bring	brought	brought
build	built	built
burn	burned	burned
buy	bought	bought
catch	caught	caught
choose	chose	chosen
come	came	come
cost	cost	cost
cut	cut	cut
do	did	done
draw	drew	drawn
drink	drank	drunk
drive	drove	driven
eat	ate	eaten
fall	fell	fallen
feel	felt	felt
find	found	found
fly	flew	flown
forget	forgot	forgotten
get	got	got/gotten
give	gave	given
go	went	gone
grow	grew	grown
have	had	had
hear	heard	heard
hide	hid	hidden
hit	hit	hit
hold	held	held
hurt	hurt	hurt
keep	kept	kept
know	knew	known

INFINITIVE	PAST TENSE	PAST/PASSIVE PARTICIPLE
learn	learned	learned
leave	left	left
lend	lent	lent
let	let	let
lose	lost	lost
make	made	made
mean	meant	meant
meet	met	met
pay	paid	paid
put	put	put
read	read	read
ring	rang	rung
run	ran	run
say	said	said
see	saw	seen
sell	sold	sold
send	sent	sent
show	showed	shown
shut	shut	shut
sing	sang	sung
sit	sat	sat
sleep	slept	slept
speak	spoke	spoken
spend	spent	spent
stand	stood	stood
steal	stole	stolen
sweep	swept	swept
swim	swam	swum
take	took	taken
teach	taught	taught
tell	told	told
think	thought	thought
throw	threw	thrown
understand	understood	understood
wake	woke	woken
wear	wore	worn
win	won	won
write	wrote	written

Appendix 4: Adjectives and adverbs

1 Comparatives and superlatives

1 We form the comparative and superlative of short adjectives (adjectives with one syllable*) with **-er** and **-est**:

cheap → *cheap**er**, the cheap**est***
long → *long**er**, the long**est***
warm → *warm**er**, the warm**est***

2 If the adjective ends in **-e**, we add **r** and **st**:

late → *late**r**, the late**st***
nice → *nice**r**, the nice**st***

3 When a one-syllable adjective ends with one vowel* and one consonant* (e.g. *big*), we double the final consonant:

big → *bi**gger**, the bi**ggest***
hot → *ho**tter**, the ho**ttest***
wet → *we**tter**, the we**ttest***

Note that we do not double **w**:

few → *few**er**, the few**est***

4 We put **more/the most** before adjectives of two or more syllables:

beautiful → ***more** beautiful, **the most** beautiful*
expensive → ***more** expensive, **the most** expensive*
polluted → ***more** polluted, **the most** polluted*

5 When an adjective ends in a consonant + -y (e.g. *happy*), the **y** changes to **-ier** or **-iest**:

dirty → *dirt**ier**, the dirt**iest***
easy → *eas**ier**, the eas**iest***
happy → *happ**ier**, the happ**iest***
lucky → *luck**ier**, the luck**iest***

6 Some adjectives have irregular comparative and superlative forms:

good → ***better, the best***
bad → ***worse, the worst***
far → ***farther, the farthest***
little → ***less, the least***

7 Be careful to use **fewer** with plural nouns (e.g. *stores*), and **less** with uncountable nouns (e.g. *money*):

*There are **fewer stores** downtown than there used to be.*
*John earns **less money** than Mary.*

2 Adverbs

1 We form most adverbs by adding **ly** to an adjective:

polite → *polite**ly***　*quick* → *quick**ly***
slow → *slow**ly***

2 When an adjective ends in a consonant + -y, the **y** changes to **-ily**:

easy → *eas**ily***　*happy* → *happ**ily***
lucky → *luck**ily***

3 When an adjective ends in a consonant + **-le**, the **e** changes to **-y**:

probable → *probab**ly***
remarkable → *remarkab**ly***

4 Some adverbs are irregular:

good → ***well***　*fast* → ***fast***
hard → ***hard***　*late* → ***late***

* Consonants: b c d f g h j k l m n p q r s t v w x y z
Vowels: a e i o u
Syllables: |*hit*| = 1 syllable, |*vi*|*sit*| = 2 syllables, |*re*|*mem*|*ber*| = 3 syllables

Answer key

Pages 2–3

A
1 visits
2 watch ✓
3 play ✓
4 go ✓
5 sings
6 eat ✓
7 sleep ✓
8 calls

B
1 owns
2 enjoys
3 finishes
4 walk
5 reads
6 teaches
7 fly

C
1 We don't speak German.
2 My dog doesn't get enough exercise.
3 He doesn't eat beef.
4 I don't play badminton.
5 You don't sing very well.
6 They don't cook often.
7 She doesn't hear the music.
8 I don't understand the question.

D
1 eat
2 brush
3 go
4 arrive
5 drink/have
6 start
7 work
8 like
9 stop
10 have/drink
11 leave
12 watch

E
1 doesn't/does not work, works
2 lives in a city, doesn't/does not live in the country
3 She speaks French. She doesn't/does not speak Japanese.
4 She doesn't/does not like surfing. She likes cycling.

Pages 4–5

A
1 ✗ They aren't eating dinner.
✓ They are relaxing.
2 ✓ I'm doing homework.
✗ I'm not talking to a friend on the phone.
3 ✓ They are playing tennis.
✗ They aren't playing soccer.
4 ✗ We aren't enjoying a day at the beach.
✓ It's raining.

B
1 are staying
2 are swimming
3 is walking
4 am sleeping
5 am taking
6 is writing
7 is shining
8 are relaxing
9 am trying

C
1 e, am walking
2 h, are taking
3 g, are cooking
4 a, is failing
5 f, is buying, is retiring
6 b, are working
7 c, is going

Pages 6–7

A
1 take
2 eats
3 are leaving
4 talk, go
5 are studying
6 walks, need
7 am, am starting
8 do you sleep
9 go, are eating
10 are you doing, need, have

B
1 is
2 ✓
3 ✓
4 lives
5 is studying
6 want
7 work
8 ✓
9 want
10 ✓
11 play
12 am writing
13 am having
14 are watching
15 do not understand
16 am
17 ✓

C
1 Suzanne is always careful when driving because she does not want to have an accident.
2 Please leave me alone! I am studying for an exam.
3 Usually I prefer to cook at home but I am too tired tonight, so we are going to a restaurant.
4 John is walking to school today although he usually takes the bus.
5 Do you speak fluent English?
6 Everyone is having fun at the party and no one wants to leave.
7 We are practising verb forms tonight because we have an exam tomorrow.
8 Jane travels every summer. Right now, she is touring South America.

Pages 8–9

A
became ✓
~~catched~~
~~talked~~
married ✓
understood ✓
~~knowed~~
~~breaked~~
played ✓
~~reminded~~
built ✓
shared ✓
brought ✓
shut ✓
~~drinked~~
sold ✓
~~freezed~~
~~thinked~~
~~taked~~
flew ✓
slept ✓
smiled ✓
~~sayed~~
worked ✓
took ✓
~~gived~~
~~forgetted~~
showed ✓
~~cutted~~
wanted ✓
~~builded~~
wrote ✓
~~hitted~~
watched ✓
~~quitted~~
thought ✓
~~swimmed~~
~~buyed~~
~~flied~~
~~selled~~
talked ✓
came ✓
knew ✓

B
1 married
2 caught, was
3 quit, got, started
4 baked, brought
5 took, didn't/did not write
6 Did you go, went
7 Did you have, shone, swam
8 Did your parents visit, came, saw

C
1 Why did you stay up so late studying?
2 I read a great book last week, but I don't remember the name of it.
3 Did you see the hockey game last night?
4 David forgot about the planes we made so he was late for dinner.
5 I sold my house in the city last year and I bought a new one in the country.
6 Mark paid for his friend's dinner, because his friend did not have his wallet.

D
1 liked
2 loved
3 Did you enjoy
4 took
5 found
6 studied
7 was
8 didn't/did not study
9 loved
10 had
11 was
12 listened
13 cleaned
14 requested
15 got
16 became

Pages 10–11

A
1 wasn't/was not listening
2 was talking
3 were waiting
4 was living
5 was coming
6 were winning
7 were sitting
8 were you staying
9 wasn't/was not driving
10 wasn't/was not raining
11 were you doing

B
1 was eating
2 were playing
3 was watching
4 was sitting
5 was writing
6 was brushing
7 was listening
8 was painting

C
1 was living
2 was studying
3 was taking
4 finished, was working
5 met, was working
6 was working, met
7 was running
8 was running, married

Pages 12–13

A
1 has been
2 has taught
3 has visited
4 has travelled
5 has worked

B
1 haven't/have not seen
2 have been
3 have you finished, haven't/have not started, have been
4 have travelled, have never visited
5 has written
6 has ever beaten
7 has made

C
1 Yes, I have visited 24 different countries.
2 But I have never spent more than two weeks in any country.
3 So you've never wanted to live abroad?
4 No, I have thought about it but I have been unsure about living so far from my family and friends.
5 I understand. I have lived in Italy, in Korea, and in Costa Rica.
6 At first it was stressful to move, but I have found it gets easier every time.
7 I have always made great friends wherever I go!

D
1 They have worked together since 1993.
2 Jack has been sick for a week.
3 Have you taken many pictures since you bought your new camera?
4 Jennifer has not seen her sister since she moved across the country.
5 I have not ridden a bike for five years.

Pages 14–15

A
1 I've/I have just come
2 I've/I have just sold
3 She's/She has just finished
4 I've/I have just gotten
5 they've/they have just moved
6 I've/I have just bought
8 I've/I have just had

B
1 Have you decided which one to buy yet?
2 I have already explained this to you three times.
3 Their baby son's/son has already started talking.
4 Have you called Lan yet?
5 The game hasn't/has not finished yet.
6 I've/I have already had lunch.
7 He's/He has already spent all his money.

C
1 Have you visited the art gallery yet?
2 I haven't/I have not done that yet
3 Have you seen a play yet?
4 I've/I have just bought a ticket
5 I've/I have already seen that play.
6 I've/I have just read
7 They've/They have just released
8 They haven't/They have not sold all the tickets yet.

Pages 16–17

A
1 went
2 saw
3 have never been
4 have heard
5 went
6 was

B
1 was
2 have been
3 have you seen
4 saw
5 failed
6 has not opened
7 has been painting
8 told
9 did
10 went

C
1 started
2 built
3 went
4 pulled
5 have opened
6 opened
7 went
8 opened
9 began
10 have built

Pages 18–19

A
1 it's/it has been raining
2 We've/We have been playing
3 Wendy's/Wendy has been studying
4 I've/I have been reading
5 We've/We have been watching
6 Have the neighbours been making
7 I've/I have been saving
8 Have you been listening

B
1 for
2 for
3 since (OR for *with a different sense*)
4 for
5 since
6 since
7 for
8 for

C
1 have been making a cake.
2 has been wrapping presents.
3 has been decorating the tree.
4 has been shopping for food.
5 has been writing cards.

D
1 It's/It has been snowing since three o'clock.
2 He's/He has been playing chess since he was ten.
3 I've/I have been working since eight o'clock.
4 Helen's/Helen has been looking for another job for two months.
5 We've/We have been waiting (here) for two hours.

Pages 20–21

A
1 had already written one article
2 had never visited Panama
3 had never read *Alice in Wonderland*
4 had already gone camping four times
5 had already made ice cream two times
6 had already worn his cowboy boots five times

B
1 When the firefighters arrived, we had already put the fire out.
2 When the manager came back, Jim had already finished the work.
3 When Philip called, I had already gone to bed.
4 When their children came home, Alice and Jack had already had lunch.
5 When his wife got home from work, Ian had already made dinner.
6 The thieves had already spent the money when the police caught them.

C
1 had filed the report
2 had seen a fox in the backyard
3 had enjoyed the hockey game
4 had made a batch of cookies
5 had finished all his homework

Pages 22–23

A
1 I'm going to write
2 I'll buy, I'll make, I'm going to meet
3 you going to compete, I'm going to decide, I'll wait
4 I'm going to wash, I'll call, I'll be
5 I'm going to go

B
1 a You look hot, I'll open a window.
2 f Thursday is no good for me, I'm afraid. I'm going to meet the new manager of our Tokyo office.
3 b Next year, we're going to enter the Japanese market.
4 c Thanks, I'll have an orange juice.
5 d Take a break. I'll do the photocopying.

C
1 No, but I'm going to see her next week.
2 Sure, I'll have some shrimp.
3 OK, I'll follow you.
4 We're going to sing karaoke.
5 Yes, I'll call you in the morning.

Pages 24–25

A
1 If you're a vegetarian, you don't eat meat.
2 If you live in a hot country, you don't like cold weather.
3 If you're a teacher, you have to work very hard.
4 If you do a lot of exercise, you stay fit and healthy.
5 If you're an environmentalist, you protect the earth.
6 If you read newspapers, you know what's happening in the world.

B
1 the weather's/is, we'll/will drive
2 she mails, they'll/will receive
3 Fiona will be, John arrives
4 I'll/will go, I have
5 she doesn't/does not pass, she won't get
6 You'll/will learn, you take
7 I get, I'll/will go
8 I'll/will buy, it doesn't/does not cost
9 you run, you'll/will catch
10 I'll/will go, I don't feel
11 they win, they'll/will be

C
1 I'll/will buy, I go
2 he doesn't call, I'll/will call
3 you want, I'll/will give
4 he'll/will fail, he doesn't work
5 you fill in, I'll/will send

Pages 26–27

A
1 until
2 when
3 When
4 after/when
5 until
6 until
7 when
8 As soon as/When
9 until
10 When
11 before
12 as soon as
13 before

B
1 'll wait, arrive
2 'll see, go
3 'll call, know
4 'll do, have
5 'll enjoy, get
6 'll tell, see
7 'll wait, comes
8 'll book, go
9 'll do, get
10 Will you see, are, 'll phone, arrive

C
1 'll/will pay
2 'll/will ask
3 has landed
4 have checked
5 'll/will read
6 have read
7 'll/will feel
8 have finished
9 'll/will be
10 have had

Pages 28–29

A
1 Neither
2 Neither
3 So
4 Neither
5 too
6 So
7 so
8 neither
9 too
10 either
11 so
12 neither

B
1 So are we.
2 Neither does mine.
3 Neither have I.
4 So was mine.
5 So has Frank.
6 Neither did George.
7 Neither can I.
8 Neither am I.
9 So did Lannie.
10 So have I.
11 So are we.
12 So is mine.

C
1 neither does
2 doesn't either
3 so does
4 does too
5 neither can
6 can't either
7 can too
8 neither can
9 so has
10 so does
11 does too
12 so does
13 neither does

Pages 30–31

A
1 for
2 to
3 for
4 –
5 –
6 –
7 –
8 on
9 –
10 with
11 for
12 to

B
1 for
2 –
3 about
4 –
5 for
6 about
7 with

C
1 What are they talking about?
2 How much is she asking for?
3 How many jobs has she applied for?
4 what are you reading?

D
1 at
2 –
3 for
4 to
5 for
6 at
7 –
8 –

Pages 32–33

A
1 get
2 make
3 have
4 had
5 done
6 get
7 have/make
8 get
9 make
10 done
11 got
12 had

B
1 had/made
2 had
3 got
4 got
5 did
6 had
7 had/made
8 done
9 did
10 made/had/got
11 did

C
1 make
2 have
3 get
4 got
5 making
6 do
7 had

Pages 34–35

A
Jack hit the ball
they play hockey
we've eaten dinner
Samantha married Michael
Janice wrote a book
I don't want to go
she is a doctor
the car is blue
no one's happy
the kids saw a movie

B
1 She is reading a book.
2 He caught a fish.
3 We have been to Paris.
4 The dog bit me.
5 Emma like to dance.
6 Mark ate a hamburger.
7 Sam is walking to school.
8 They are learning English.
9 The girls are teaching them.
10 Sarah played guitar.
11 We want a vacation.
12 The kids are tired.

C
1 We drove home together after school.
2 We did not share the sandwich.
3 ✓
4 Marie is not having fun.
5 ✓

D
1 Her dad her bought a new car.
2 I made you a cup of tea.
3 Vish baked his grandma cookies yesterday.
4 Everyone is sending Daryl a birthday card.
5 The class is buying the teacher a present.
6 Janice gave the dog a treat.
7 She is not leaving her husband a note.
8 Khalida is writing her sister an email.

E
1 Justin doesn't play football anymore.
2 Max is visiting Paris next summer.
3 I sent you flowers on your birthday.
4 David wrote Sonya a letter yesterday.
5 The book was excellent.
6 My parents took a vacation last month.
7 She is buying her friend a gift.
8 Sue told me a beautiful story.
9 I read that book quickly.
10 Both my brothers are studying Spanish at school.
11 My mom made chicken soup for me when I was sick.
12 Nicole was excited about the trip.
13 I mailed you a letter yesterday.
14 The boys are hungry.

Pages 36–37

A
1 Who wants some more coffee?
2 What happened at the end of the story?
3 Who is going to pay the bill?
4 What did he have for breakfast?
5 What did their letter say?
6 Who knows the answer to my question?
7 What did they see?
8 Who is she calling?

B
1 Who went on the trip?
2 What's happening in this movie?
3 Who are you going to call?
4 What did you watch on TV last night?
5 Who sent these flowers?
6 What did you buy in that store?
7 What has made Ray so happy?

C
1 What happened?
2 Who took his driving test?
3 What did Robert fail?
4 What did Robert say to Philip?
5 Who met Linda for coffee?

D
1 won the Nobel Prize
2 did Bell invent
3 climbed Everest
4 did Prince William marry
5 destroyed Hiroshima
6 did Gretzky play

Pages 38–39

A
1 How often does he read a newspaper?
2 How much does a single room cost?
3 How old were you when you went to live in Montreal?
4 How many courses are you going to take?
5 How long will the course last?
6 How far is it from here to the nearest bus stop?

B
1 How many languages do/can you speak?
2 How far is it from here to the airport?
3 How much did the meal cost?
4 How long did you stay there?
5 How often does the delivery man come?
6 How much cheese did you buy?

C
1 from, to
2 every
3 much
4 from, to
5 years old
6 many

D
Possible answers:
1 How often do you go there?
2 How long do the classes last?
3 How often do you study at home?
4 How many people are (there) in your class?
5 How old are they?
6 How far is it from your home?
7 How much does it cost?

Pages 40–41

A
1 don't you
2 isn't it
3 does it
4 don't they
5 have you
6 aren't you

B
1 can't I
2 will it
3 was he
4 did I
5 will it
6 wasn't it
7 can you
8 didn't they

C
1 isn't it?
2 haven't you?
3 can you?
4 don't they?
5 won't I?

D
1 speak French (very well), can't you?
2 heard this story, have you?
3 to Frank's party, didn't you?
4 very far from here, is it?
5 be angry, will she?
6 going to leave now, are you?
7 be at home tonight, won't you?

Pages 42–43

A
1 must not call
2 You must leave
3 You must wipe
4 You must not use
5 You must pay

B
1 You must bring
2 You must not talk
3 You must show
4 You must wipe
5 You must not leave

C
1 I must not dance all night.
2 I must run every morning.
3 I must not sleep in the afternoon.
4 I must not watch TV all day.
5 I must visit my grandmother.
6 I must study in the evening.

D
1 must not tell lies
2 must not open the door
3 must go out for dinner with us
4 must show identity cards
5 must not eat
6 must follow the instructions

Pages 44–45

A
1 don't have to be polite
2 have to be polite
3 have to work
4 don't have to work
5 have to wear
6 don't have to wear

B
1 I didn't have to work
2 Do I have to do OR Have I got to do
3 I had to run
4 I had to go
5 Did you have to show
6 Do/Will I have to pay OR Have I got to pay
7 do you have to have OR have you got to have
8 You don't/won't have to decide OR You haven't got to decide
9 I had to wait
10 Do you have to work, I had to work

C
1 You have to fill in an application form. OR You've got to fill in an application form.
2 Do I have to give you a photograph? OR Have I got to give you a photograph?

3 No, you don't have to give me anything, except the money for the card. OR No, you haven't got to give me anything, etc.
4 We had to do some French tests.
5 How many questions did you have to answer?
6 We had to answer about forty grammar questions.
7 I had to think about them very carefully.
8 Did you have to write an essay?
9 No, but we have to do one next week. OR No, but we have got to do one next week.

Pages 46–47

A
1 You shouldn't park
2 should I cook
3 You should wear
4 You shouldn't smoke
5 We should arrive
6 Should I pay
7 I should apply
8 I should write
9 I shouldn't eat
10 We should complain
11 I should buy

B
1 You should cut
2 You should use
3 You shouldn't add
4 You should wait
5 You should heat
6 You should cut

C
1 Which papers should I get?
2 I think you should buy the local newspapers.
3 What do you think I should do before I buy a bike?
4 I don't think you should decide too quickly.
5 You should check the condition of the bike.
6 You should ask somebody who knows about bikes to look at the bike for you.
7 You shouldn't buy one simply because it looks nice!
8 You should be very careful.

Pages 48–49

A
1 May I please have a glass of orange juice? OR May I have a glass of orange juice, please?
2 Can we watch that movie?
3 Can I please use your cellphone? OR Can I use your cellphone, please?
4 May I borrow your camera tomorrow?
5 Could you please pass the maple syrup? OR Could you pass the maple syrup, please?
6 Can you mail this letter for me?

B
1 May I use your computer?
2 Can I see the newspaper, please?
3 May I borrow your notes?
4 Can I have the window seat, please?

C
1 Could you switch seats with me?
2 Could you heat this up, please?
3 Could you lend me five dollars?
4 Could you turn up the heat, please?

D
1 could
2 Can't, may
3 Could, can't
4 Could, can, can't

Pages 50–51

A
1 was told
2 was written
3 was bitten
4 are paid
5 is watched
6 was sold
7 was found
8 was given

B
1 was Sophia told not to do?
2 was *The Handmaid's Tale* written?
3 was bitten by a snake while you were hiking?
4 are firefighters paid by?
5 people is this show watched by every week?
6 did his painting sell for?
7 was this wallet found?
8 were you given a speeding ticket?

C
1 This ruby bracelet was given to me by Muni.
2 A vegetable garden was planted by Jeff.
3 Garbage isn't collected on weekends.
4 This fence was painted white.
5 The baby was picked up by a nurse.
6 This letter was written last week.

D
1 produced
2 were exported
3 started
4 were tested
5 was called
6 exported
7 are sold

Pages 52–53

A
1 stop running
2 don't mind listening
3 keeps losing
4 enjoys going, likes meeting
5 keep making
6 finish eating
7 doesn't enjoy driving, loves cycling

B
1 like living
2 would like to be
3 don't like getting up
4 would like to go out
5 would like to find
6 don't like watching
7 likes lying

C
1 he went dancing.
2 he went cycling.
3 he went swimming.
4 he went skiing.
5 he went sailing.

D
1 Playing
2 Driving
3 Eating

Pages 54–55

A
1 to call
2 be
3 clean
4 enjoy
5 to wait
6 to eat
7 reply
8 feel
9 drive
10 to bring
11 receive

B
1 go to the meeting on Friday.
2 to meet some friends tonight.
3 to listen to what I'm telling you.
4 to lock the door when you go out.
5 go out for dinner tonight.
6 me pay for the meal.
7 to take a course in art history.
8 to pay the bill.
9 to sit in this chair?
10 me laugh a lot.
11 call you tomorrow.
12 be angry with you.
13 me drive her new car.

C
1 do
2 to go
3 to come
4 to leave
5 to start
6 to take
7 to reach
8 meet
9 be

Pages 56–57

A
1 (that) she was going to a conference.
2 (that) he'd/he had lost his passport.
3 (that) they'd/they had been on holiday.
4 (that) she didn't understand.

B
1 (that) it had rained
2 (that) she had bought, (that) she rode
3 (that) she had not been
4 (that) she was going to go
5 (that) Rosie could go
6 (that) she would meet
7 (that) they would be

C
1 told
2 said
3 said
4 told
5 told
6 said
7 told
8 said
9 said
10 told

Pages 58–59

A
1 a, —
2 the
3 —, a, the, —
4 an
5 —, —
6 the, The

B
1 the, —
2 the
3 a, —
4 —, —
5 —
6 a
7 the
8 the, the
9 a
10 —, —

C
1 an
2 a
3 —
4 the
5 a
6 a
7 —
8 a
9 the
10 a
11 the
12 —

D
1 a
2 the
3 The
4 a
5 the
6 an
7 a
8 the
9 a

Pages 60–61

A
1 himself
2 myself
3 ourselves
4 themselves
5 himself
6 himself

B
1 enjoyed ourselves very much.
2 burnt myself
3 He taught himself.
4 I think I'm going to buy/I'll buy myself a new coat tomorrow.
5 She made herself a sandwich

C
1 myself
2 herself
3 themselves
4 ourselves
5 himself

D
1 You'll have to mail it yourself.
2 we carried all our luggage ourselves.
3 Did you take it yourself?
4 she (had) made herself.
5 I chose it myself.
6 I invented the recipe myself.

E
1 each other
2 each other
3 yourself/yourselves
4 ourselves
5 each other
6 each other

Pages 62–63

A
1 She offered Jim a mint.
2 He showed Juliette his vacation photos.
3 Have you sent them an invitation?
4 Did you buy her a birthday present?
5 I gave a friend some of my books.
6 When you go to the post office, could you get me some stamps?

B
1 She offered a mint to Jim.
2 He showed his vacation photos to Juliette.
3 Have you sent an invitation to them?
4 Did you buy a birthday present for her?
5 I gave some of my books to a friend.
6 When you go to the post office, could you get some stamps for me?

C
1 They sent us an invitation.
2 Sheila gave a present to Mike.
3 I made her a sandwich.
4 Donald bought a newspaper for Sally.
5 My uncle sold me his camera.
6 She left a message for you.
7 Isabel sent them some flowers.
8 Did you take the money to the bank?

D
1 The waiter got them some wine.
The waiter got some wine for them.
2 The waiter showed him the bottle.
The waiter showed the bottle to Rob.
3 The chef cooked them a special meal.
The chef cooked a special meal for them.
4 The waiter gave Rob the bill.
The waiter gave the bill to Rob.
5 Jen lent Rob some money, because he didn't have enough to pay the bill.
Jen lent some money to Rob, because he didn't have enough to pay the bill.

Pages 64–65

A
1 Somebody
2 somewhere
3 anyone
4 everything
5 something
6 nothing
7 everywhere
8 somebody
9 Everyone, nobody

B
1 knew
2 haven't seen
3 didn't eat
4 has happened
5 is
6 didn't say

C
1 anything interesting
2 anywhere else
3 anywhere cheap
4 somewhere else
5 something hot

D
1 somebody (OR someone)
2 somebody (OR someone)
3 everywhere
4 something
5 everything
6 anybody (OR anyone)
7 nowhere
8 anything
9 something
10 something

Pages 66–67

A
1 ✓
2 Each assignment on the course has to
3 ✓
4 every parking lot was full.
5 ✓
6 each of them lasts

B
1 other
2 others
3 other
4 another
5 another

C
1 other
2 Another
3 other
4 another
5 Other
6 one

D
1 the other
2 other, other
3 others
4 One, the other
5 another

Pages 68–69

A
1 all of the
2 none of
3 some of the
4 some of
5 some of
6 none of
7 none of the
8 all of the

B
1 all
2 All the (OR Some of the)
3 Some
4 None of the
5 all
6 None of the
7 all
8 all
9 none of the
10 All the
11 Some
12 some of the

C
1 Most professional athletes are paid well and some of them are very rich.
2 Most of the ocean is very salty and none of it is fresh water.
3 Some current music is very good but some of it is terrible.
4 Most Indian food is spicy and some of it is very spicy.
5 All of my relatives are slim and none of them is/are very tall.
6 Most of my friends are students but none of them is/are very smart.
7 Most of Nepal is mountainous and none of it is flat.
8 Most of the earth is covered in water but some of it is desert.

Pages 70–71

A
1 like
2 as
3 like
4 As
5 as
6 like

B
1 as
2 like
3 like
4 as
5 like
6 as
7 like
8 as

C
1 like
2 As
3 like
4 as if/as though
5 Like
6 like
7 As

D
1 like
2 like
3 as
4 As
5 as
6 as if/as though/like
7 as if/as though/like
8 as

Pages 72–73

A
1 as quickly as
2 as angry as
3 as expensive as
4 as big as
5 as good as
6 as hard as

B
1 as fast as
2 as tall as
3 as long as
4 as clean as
5 as fresh as
6 as full as
7 as strong as
8 as wide as
9 as big as

C
1 as much (money) as
2 as many countries as
3 as many jobs as
4 as much luggage as
5 as many questions as
6 as much (money) as

Pages 74–75

A
1 too dark
2 enough information
3 too late
4 enough food
5 too nervous
6 too fast
7 good enough
8 enough clothes
9 well enough
10 strong enough
11 too cold
12 enough stamps

B
1 enough time
2 too many questions
3 warm enough
4 too much salt
5 enough questions
6 too many people
7 comfortable enough
8 too much noise
9 enough players
10 enough bread
11 too many mistakes

C
1 I'm too tired to do any more work.
2 Heidi isn't smart enough to pass the exam.
3 Clive is too short to play basketball. (OR Clive isn't tall enough to play basketball.)
4 His girlfriend was too sick to go to the party. (OR His girlfriend wasn't well enough to go to the party.)
5 David didn't have enough money to pay the bill.
6 Is it hot enough to go to the beach?
7 I'm too busy to see you tonight.
8 It's too early (for me) to go home.
9 Chris didn't have enough tools to fix the car.
10 I didn't have enough time to visit all the museums.

Pages 76–77

A
1 excited
2 surprised
3 interesting
4 tiring
5 surprised
6 bored
7 exciting
8 boring

B
1 amusing
2 boring
3 interested
4 confusing
5 bored
6 amused
7 confused
8 surprising
9 surprised

C
1 entertaining
2 interesting
3 confusing
4 frightened
5 bored
6 boring
7 surprising
8 convincing
9 disappointed
10 convinced
11 relaxed
12 surprised

Pages 78–79

A
1 outside
2 out
3 nearby
4 upstairs
5 forward
6 away
7 away
8 abroad

B
1 Turn left OR Turn right
2 straight ahead
3 Turn right OR Turn left
4 on the right

C
1 *Then/Next/Secondly/ After that* I made a list of apartments I could afford.
2 *Then/Next/Thirdly/ After that* I went to see some of the apartments.
3 *Then/Next/After that* I decided which apartment to rent.
4 *Then/Next/After that* I agreed with the landlord that I would rent it.
5 *Then/Next/After that* I signed the lease.
6 *Then/Next/After that* I paid the last month's rent as a deposit.
7 *Then/After that/ Afterwards/Finally/ Lastly* I moved into the apartment.

Pages 80–81

A
1 fairly
2 fairly
3 really
4 really
5 fairly
6 fairly
7 really
8 fairly
9 really
10 fairly

B
1 a pleasant, sunny day
2 a nice big smile
3 a large black coffee
4 a dirty old coat
5 a large white building
6 a big brown moose
7 a tall thin woman
8 a small blue car
9 a strange little story

C
1 a coffee pot
2 a photo album
3 a tennis court
4 a street sign
5 a door handle
6 a flight attendant
7 a stereo system
8 a phone book
9 a coat hanger
10 a paper cup
11 a soup bowl

Pages 82–83

A
1 ✓
2 on
3 in front of
4 ✓
5 in
6 ✓
7 ✓
8 behind

B
1 at
2 at, in
3 on
4 on
5 in
6 at/in

C
1 into, out of, into
2 onto, into, off, onto

D
1 from
2 across
3 along
4 past
5 up
6 in front of
7 down
8 through
9 under

Pages 84–85

A
1 with
2 with
3 in
4 with
5 in
6 with
7 with

8 in
9 in
10 with
11 with
12 in
13 with
14 in

B
1 with (l)
2 with (m)
3 with (k)
4 with (i)
5 with (d)
6 with (c)
7 with (f)
8 with (a)
9 by (h)
10 in (j)
11 with (o)
12 with (b)
13 without (n)
14 with (e)

C
1 He fixed the car by changing some of the parts.
2 She answered the question without reading it carefully.
3 He left without saying thank you.
4 She got the money by selling her car.
5 I deleted the email without reading it.
6 We worked all day without eating anything.
7 He lost weight by going on a strict diet.
8 I went out without locking the door.

Pages 86–87

A
1 but, so
2 so, but
3 but, so
4 so, but
5 so, but
6 but, so

B
1 Rebecca plays both hockey and softball.
2 This book is both long and boring.
3 I am going to both New York and Boston this summer.
4 Both my niece and my nephew are very active children.

C
1 Maria is either going to study law or medicine. OR Maria is going to study either law or medicine.
2 You have either the flu or a cold.
3 He is either sick or on vacation.
4 I am either going skiing at Banff or Tremblant. OR I am going skiing either at Banff or Tremblant.

D
1 Neither my mom nor my dad has ever been to Europe.
2 Neither the beach nor the lake is clean.
3 Neither Annie nor Joe is happy about the decision.
4 Neither the kids nor the adults liked the restaurant.

E
1 neither of us
2 either of them
3 both of us, neither of us
4 both of them
5 both of them, either of them
6 neither of them

Pages 88–89

A
1 that
2 they
3 ✓
4 ✓
5 that, it
6 ✓
7 who are

B
1 Is this the bus that goes to Red Deer?
2 The woman who was talking to our class was wearing a blue shirt.
3 ✓
4 ✓
5 Do you know anyone who plays basketball?
6 This is the cake that tastes like lemon.
7 ✓

C
1 Will acted in
2 Ellissa designed
3 who makes the decisions
4 that produces microchips
5 who plays soccer

D
1 that fits in my backpack
2 that will light even if they get wet
3 we use at home for lighting candles
4 that keeps the bears away
5 I baked myself
6 I asked you to buy at the grocery store
7 we could go fishing for food
8 that were in the garage
9 we'll have to drive to the nearest town

Pages 90–93 (Review test)

The number after each answer indicates the page number on which you can find information about that grammar point.

1 b 2
2 d 4
3 a 6
4 a 8
5 d 10
6 a 12
7 d 14
8 b 16
9 c 16
10 c 18
11 b 20
12 c 22
13 d 24
14 a 26
15 d 28
16 a 30
17 a 30
18 c 32
19 b 34
20 c 36
21 d 38
22 d 40
23 b 42
24 a 44
25 b 46
26 a 48
27 c 50
28 a 52
29 b 54
30 d 54
31 d 56
32 a 58
33 c 58
34 a 60
35 a 62
36 c 64
37 a 66
38 d 68
39 c 70
40 b 72
41 d 74
42 c 76
43 b 78
44 c 80
45 b 82
46 b 82
47 c 82
48 b 84
49 c 86
50 c 88
51 c 88
52 b 88

Index